# BASIC
# Programming
# for Business

# BASIC
# Programming
# for Business

Irvine H. Forkner

Metropolitan State College
Denver, Colorado

**PRENTICE-HALL, INC.**
Englewood Cliffs, New Jersey  07632

Library of Congress Cataloging in Publication Data

Forkner, Irvine, (date)
  Basic programming for business.

  Includes index.
  1. Basic (Computer program language). I. Title.
HF5548.5.B3F67 1977    001.6'424    77-23145
ISBN 0-13-066423-5

Printed in the United States of America

10  9  8  7  6

Prentice-Hall International, Inc., *London*
Prentice-Hall of Australia Pty. Limited, *Sydney*
Prentice-Hall of Canada, Ltd., *Toronto*
Prentice-Hall of India Private Limited, *New Delhi*
Prentice-Hall of Japan, Inc., *Tokyo*
Prentice-Hall of Southeast Asia Pte. Ltd., *Singapore*
Whitehall Books Limited, *Wellington, New Zealand*

To my wife and daughter
Mary Jane and Sue

# Contents

# Preface

The major purpose of BASIC Programming for Business is to help students of business develop programming skills that will enable them to use a computer in the context of business rather than mathematics or science.

A second purpose is to develop an understanding and appreciation of the electronic computer, its capabilities and limitations, the concepts of computer problem solving, and the concepts of programming languages.

The author believes that the student should develop a fundamental programming capability as soon as possible; that he should begin writing and running programs immediately. Therefore, Chapter 1 of this text presents sufficient input, process, and output statements so that this goal is accomplished.

The BASIC statements are presented in the context of simple business problems. The student can therefore focus his efforts on learning BASIC and not on deciphering the problem and its solution algorithm.

BASIC is rapidly becoming an almost universal programming language because:

1- BASIC is an extremely simple yet powerful programming language. Because of its simplicity, the student is able to concentrate on problem solutions rather than language syntax.

2- more and more business managers, mathematicians, scientists, engineers, educators, and students

are recognizing the superiority of the computer
as an analytical tool.

3-  the "state of the art" in managerial decision
    making requires an analytical sophistication
    that can only be obtained through the use of a
    computer.

4-  both batch and timeshare BASIC compilers are
    available for most computer systems including
    minicomputers.

This text may be used in a first programming course
or as a supplement to an introduction to data processing,
or a first quantitative methods course.  It may be used
with or without formal instruction either in a batch or
an interactive terminal environment.

# BASIC
# Programming
# for Business

# 1

# Basic BASIC

INTRODUCTION

BASIC is a computer programming language.  A computer
program is a set of instructions that tells the computer to
do certain jobs.  Your job is to learn how to write these
instructions in BASIC.  BASIC (Beginners All-purpose Symbolic
Instruction Code) is a special language that you will use to
create computer programs so that you may tell your computer
to solve different kinds of business problems.

> Your computer speaks BASIC.  To you it is
> a foreign language, but you too can learn
> to speak BASIC.

The advantages of BASIC are (1) it is easy to learn
and use, (2) it is very powerful mathematically, and (3) it
is therefore a very useful tool that you can use to solve business
problems calling for mathematical processes.

When you have mastered the material in this chapter,
you will be able to speak BASIC to your computer.  You will
be able to tell it to

1- Enter data into the system.

2- Process these data.

3- Make decisions about these data.

4- Print out the answer you want.

> After you have mastered basic BASIC, you
> may wish to use some of the standard functions
> presented in Chapter 6.

1

PROGRAMMING CONCEPTS

A computer program is a group or set of statements.
Each statement or instruction tells the computer what to do.
For example, you can write an instruction that tells the
computer to add two numbers together and to save the answer.
But when the instruction is carried out depends on the
order of the instructions within the program.  The computer
executes or carries out these instructions in the same order
in which they are received by the computer.

You must, therefore, give the instructions to the
computer in the same order in which you want the computer
to execute them, or you will not get the answer you want.

> Your computer can do only one thing at a time.
> And it does what you tell it to do only in the
> order or sequence you decree.

The idea of sequence is found in many noncomputer jobs.
For instance, a check-out clerk in a grocery store must
follow a set sequence of operations to determine the amount
owed by a customer, as follows:

1- Read the price of an item.

2- Enter the price of that item into the cash register
(add up or sum all prices).

3- If there are more items, return to Step 1.  If there
aren't any more, continue to Step 4.

4- Depress the TOTAL key.  The cash register will show
the total amount owed in the "window."

5- Collect the amount owed from the customer.

If we were to computerize the grocery check-out steps,
we would have to program the computer so that it would do
these same steps in a sequence very similar to that shown
above.  We could not, for example, collect the total amount
owed from the customer (Step 5) without first finding the

sum of prices for all items. And we could not sum the
prices (Step 2) without first reading the price of each item.

Let's look at another example of this step-by-step process. We want to set up a management control procedure to
ensure payroll accuracy. We want to calculate the gross pay
for each hourly paid employee and accumulate those totals.
Later, we will compare this total with the total computed
during the regular payroll run. If these totals are equal,
we will know that our actual payroll is correct. The
step-by-step sequence we need to follow to calculate the
total pay for all employees is

     1- Read hours worked and pay rate.

     2- If hours worked are more than 40, skip to Step 5.
        If not, continue to Step 3.

     3- Calculate gross pay for regular time.

     4- Skip to Step 6.

     5- Calculate gross pay for regular plus overtime hours.

     6- Accumulate gross pay amounts.

     7- If there are more data to be read and processed,
        return to Step 1.

     8- Print out the total for all employees.

     9- END OF JOB

Remember that your computer can do only one little job
at a time. Notice that each step shown above describes just
one job and that the sequence is in a logical order. You
should observe that these steps are carried out in a set
sequence unless there is an IF or a SKIP step. These steps
change the normal step-by-step sequence and are essential to
the correct solution of our problem.

> Actually, these steps can be translated directly
> into BASIC and fed to your computer along with the
> appropriate data. You will do this later.

Now It's Your Turn

> You will find these exercises throughout the
> book.  You will notice that a problem or
> question is given and space for your answer.
> The space is followed by five *'s.  Before you
> start to read the problem, you should cover the
> page with a piece of paper or your hand and
> move your cover down to the first *****.  Then
> answer the question, uncover the suggested
> answer, and check your answer.  If your answer
> is OK, go on to the next problem or next
> section.  If you goofed, study the suggested
> answer, or go back in the text until you
> understand your error and can remember not to
> do that again.  Then go on the the next
> question.

1-   One of the processes you need to do to reconcile your
checking account statement each month is to add up all the
outstanding checks.  (If you don't know what an outstanding
check is, you are in trouble.  So I will tell you and get you
out of trouble!  It is a check that you have written against
your account but which has not been processed by your bank
as yet.)

     Now that we know where we are, I want you to write down
the steps that you would follow to add up all your outstanding
checks on an adding machine.

     1- _____
     2- _____
     3- _____
     4- _____
     5- _____
     6- _____
*****

Your steps should look something like this:
1-  Clear the adding machine.
2-  Read an amount from a check.
3-  Enter that amount into the adding machine.
4-  Push the "plus" key.

5-  If there are more checks, return to Step 2.  If not,
continue to Step 6.

6-  Push the "total" key.

Your steps could be different from these, but if you combined
Steps 2 and 3 or forgot to return to Step 2, you should start
thinking in smaller pieces, the way a computer does.

A Computer System

Just exactly what is a computer?  It is a group of
machines that are designed to process data.  A typical
computer system consists of two or three separate machines
or devices.  Figure 1-1 shows a two-device computer system.

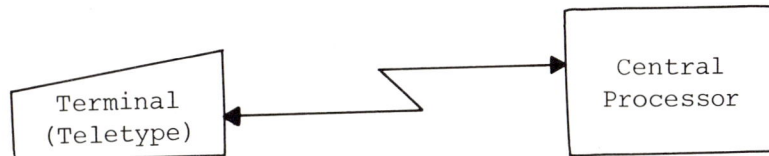

Figure 1-1

Two-Device Computer System

The two-device system consists of an input/output
terminal and a central processor, which are usually connected
by telephone lines.  The input/output device has a keyboard similar to a typewriter.  You type your programs and
data on the keyboard, and these are sent to the central
processor.  The processor controls the system and carries
out the program instructions as you typed them.  The
answer is then sent back to the terminal where it is
printed out or displayed on a TV-like screen.

Figure 1-2 shows a three-device computer system.

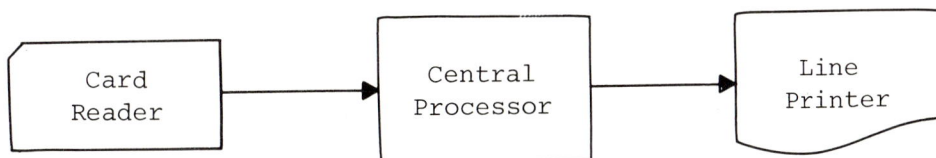

Figure 1-2

Three-Device Computer System

The input in the three-device system is performed by the card reader.  This machine interprets the holes punched in cards which are produced by a separate machine called a keypunch machine.

---

A keypunch is a typewriter-like machine that you use to punch holes in cards.  These holes represent your program instructions and problem data.

---

The card reader sends these program instructions and data to the central processor, which does the same job as in the two-device system.  Your answer is then printed out on the line printer.

As stated above, the central processor controls the system and carries out or executes the program instructions. The central processor also provides many storage cells in which your program is stored while it is being executed. Other storage cells are used to store the problem data as they are sent from the input device to the central processor. The processor then makes the needed calculations as stated in the program and stores the answers in still other storage cells.  The answers are then sent from their storage cells to the output device where they are printed for human use.

There are other computer system configurations, but all of them include some way to enter programs and data, an input device; a central processor; and some way to produce your answers, an output device.

## Parts of a Computer Program

Most computer programs will include four parts:  input, transfer, process, and output.  The input part of the program supplies data to the computer.  The data may be the numbers needed for the solution of a problem.  In the grocery check-out example we discussed earlier, the prices of the items were the data.  In the payroll example, the hours worked and the pay rate for each employee were the data.

One <u>transfer</u> or branch part of the program asks a question and causes the computer to make a decision to perhaps change the program sequence.  This is called a <u>conditional</u> transfer.  The computer usually answers the question with a "yes" or "no."  If the answer is "yes," the sequence of the program is changed by transferring control to another point in the program.  If the answer is "no," the computer continues with the sequence as written.  In the grocery check-out example, Step 3 asks if there are more items.  If the answer is "yes," the sequence is changed and control is transferred to Step 1.  If the answer is "no," the computer continues to Step 4.

A second transfer part of a program is called an <u>unconditional</u> <u>transfer</u>.  This transfer causes the computer to change the program sequence without question.  Step 4 in the payroll program is an example of an unconditional transfer.  This statement causes the computer to jump over Step 5 and to go directly to Step 6.  (Do not pass GO.)

There is an interesting conditonal transfer in the payroll program at Step 7.  You should notice that this step causes the computer to branch back to Step 1 if there are more employee data.  This kind of transfer causes the steps in the program to be repeated over and over again and is called a <u>loop</u>.  This is one of the most powerful programming tools.

The <u>process</u> part of a program usually makes calculations. The addition or summing of the prices of each item in the check-out example is a process of calculating.  Other calculations may be subtraction, multiplication, and division.  There are three processes in the payroll example. Can you identify them?

> The first is to calculate gross pay for regular time.  The second calculates gross pay for regular time plus overtime, and the third adds up all the gross pay amounts.

The <u>output</u> part of the program gives the answer to the
problem.  The answer may be a total as in the check-out
example, or it may be one of many payroll checks in a
complete payroll program.

Figure 1-3 shows the relationship among these four parts
of a simple program.  The words within each symbol are the
key words used in BASIC to tell the computer what to do.

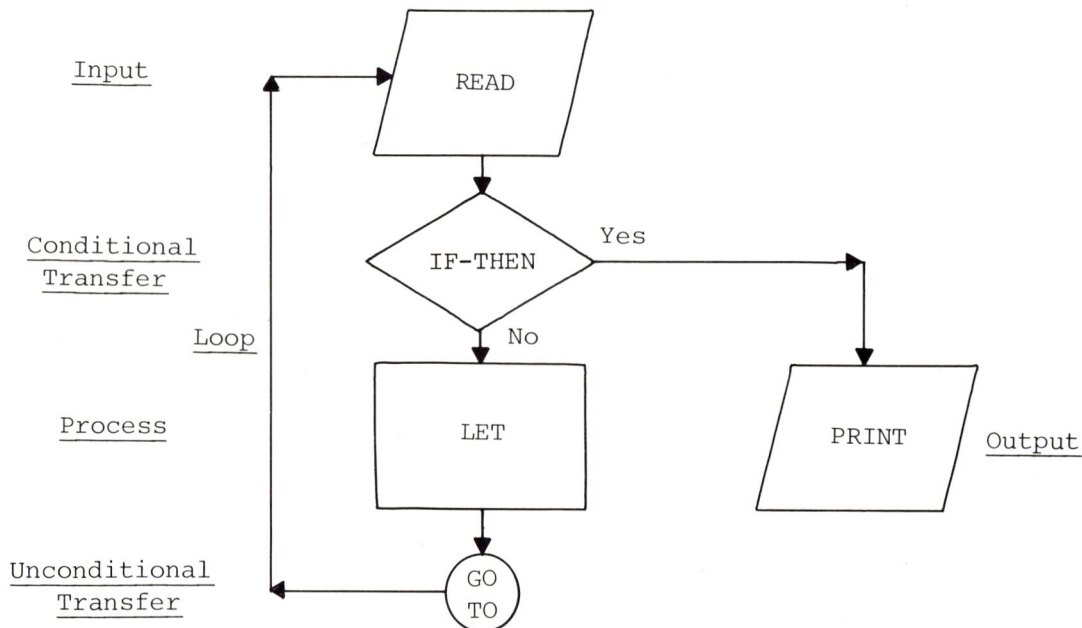

Figure 1-3

Four Parts of a Simple Computer Program

In Figure 1-3, a parallelogram is used to represent the
input part of your program.  The READ statement is the BASIC
translation of that symbol.  This statement enters data into
the <u>central processing unit</u> (CPU) and causes the computer to
save these data for you.  After the data are entered, you
may cause the data to be printed.

The diamond-shaped symbol in Figure 1-3 represents the
<u>conditional transfer</u> part of your program.  The IF-THEN
statement is used to cause the computer to make a decision.
This statement asks a question.  If the answer is "yes," the
program changes sequence as shown in Figure 1-3.  However,
if the answer is "no," the program continues with the
sequence as programmed.

The rectangle represents a <u>process</u>.  You usually ask the computer to do arithmetic in the process part of your program, using a LET statement.

The arrow pointing to the left and back to the beginning of the diagram in Figure 1-3 usually represents an <u>unconditional transfer</u> within a program.  The GO TO in the small circle is not usually included in this kind of diagram.  However, you use the GO TO statement to tell the computer to make an unconditional branch.

The <u>output</u> part of your program is also represented by a parallelogram.  You will tell the computer to display your answers using the PRINT statement.  The output may be printed on paper or may show on a TV-like tube.

This kind of diagram is called a <u>program flowchart,</u> and it is used to make a graphic plan of the sequence of steps needed to solve a problem.

<u>Programming Steps</u>

You should try to follow these eight steps when using your computer to solve problems:

1- Study the problem.  Decide what output you need or want.  Then decide what input you must have and what processes and transfers you must use to produce your output.

2- Plan a solution.  Use a program flowchart to graph the sequence of the solution.

3- Code the computer program.  Follow the sequence you planned in your program flowchart.  Usually, you write one BASIC statement for each flowchart symbol, and the shape of the symbol gives you a clue to which BASIC statement to use.

4- Convert your BASIC program into computer-usable form.  (Your computer cannot read printed material.)  If you are using a three-device computer system (punched cards), keypunch one card for each BASIC statement.  (See Appendix A for keypunch operating instructions.)

5- Enter your program into the computer.  "Feed" your

punched card deck into the card reader and it will be
stored in the central processor.

---

You will need to include some "control"
cards so that your computer will know
what to do with your deck of cards.  See
Appendix B for an example of job control
cards used for one popular computer system.

---

OR

"Log on," using a terminal; then type one line for
each BASIC statement.

---

There are different "log on" procedures for
different computer systems.  See Appendix C for
an example.

---

6-  Correct (debug) any programming errors.  Your
    computer will usually print out your program just
    as you entered it.  If you made any keypunch,
    typing, and/or programming language errors, your
    computer will tell you about them.  You make
    corrections by repunching any incorrect cards or
    retyping any incorrect lines on your terminal.
    (Do it right this time.)
        After you have corrected your errors, your
    program should "run" at Step 5.  (See Appendix D
    for debugging techniques.)

7-  Test your answer with sample data.  You should
    make up test data and feed them to your computer.
    Then compare the answer you get from your computer
    with an answer you calculate by hand.  If the two
    answers are the same, you can assume your program
    is OK.  If they are different, something is wrong
    somewhere.  "Back to the drawing board."

> In the "real" world, this is a most important step.  Your boss isn't going to tell you the right answer.  He won't know.

8-  Run the program, using "real" data.  In actual practice, you will write and test a program and then use it over and over again.  For instance, you may write a payroll program and then use it each week for a year or more before you have to modify that program.  But, in the classroom, you will write a program, test it, run it, and get the right answer, turn it in to your instructor, and that program will never be used again.

Now It's Your Turn

1-  Identify the devices in a two-device computer system.

_____

_____

_____

*****

   If you couldn't remember, you should have checked back to Figure 1-1.  You should have written

Terminal or teletype_____

Central processor_____

_____

2-  Identify the input and output devices for a three-device computer system.

_____

_____

*****

   Check your answers with Figure 1-2.

3-  What are the four parts of a computer program?

_____,  _____, _____, _____,

*****

I hope you didn't have to go back to page 6 to find the answer.  Input, transfer, process, and output are what you should have put down.

4-  Which part of a computer program is represented by the diamond-shaped symbol?  Be specific.

_____

*****

Conditional transfer is the correct answer.  If you just wrote transfer, you get only half a point.

5-  Which BASIC statement would you use to tell the computer to do some arithmetic?

_____

*****

You should have put down LET.  If you missed this one, I strongly urge you to return to the discussion of Figure 1-3 and memorize those symbols and the BASIC statements that are used for each symbol.

CODING RULES FOR BASIC

One coding rule that is required in BASIC is that each program statement must be preceded by a line or sequence number.  These numbers tell the computer what sequence to follow.  In most systems, the statements must be physically entered in the same sequence as the line numbers.  The line numbers must be whole numbers and may range from 1 to 99999.

> Some computer systems allow only four-digit
> line numbers.  I suggest, therefore, that you
> write your programs with no more than four digit
> line numbers.

You may not repeat a line number within a program, and the line numbers must be in ascending order.  Your first statement will have the smallest line number, and the END statement, always the last one, will have the highest number.

Your line numbers need not follow any special pattern, such as 1, 2, 3, 4, ... or 5, 10, 15, 20, ..., 1000.  For

instance, this set of line numbers is correct: 1, 2, 30, 55,
501, 502, ..., 900.

> Notice the gaps between these line numbers: 5,
> 10, 15, etc. Sometines, after you have written
> a program, you will want to add a statement.
> You may use one of the "missing" numbers for
> your added statement and still keep the line
> numbers in ascending order.

Another BASIC coding rule is that a statement and its
line number may not go beyond 72 spaces on the teletype or
72 punched card columns.  The computer ignores any
characters in a statement that occur after the 72nd column.

SAMPLE PROBLEM

The problem you wish to solve is to calculate the total
amount one customer owes for groceries.  This is the grocery
check-out system we talked about before.  We can follow the
programming steps listed on page 9.

1- Study the problem.  The required output is the total
   amount owed by one customer.  Therefore, you need to
   input the price of each item.  There is only one
   process, to add up or accumulate the prices of all
   items.  One conditional transfer is needed, to
   decide if there are more items.  And we need an
   unconditional transfer to close the loop so that we
   may process all the grocery items.

2- Plan a solution.  Figure 1-4 is a program flowchart
   showing the sequence of steps needed for the
   solution.  You should notice that we have changed
   the sequence slightly because the computer cannot
   actually look to see if all the items have been
   processed.  We have to ask the computer to input a
   "dummy" price after it has processed all real prices.
   Then we tell the computer to decide if a price is the
   dummy price.

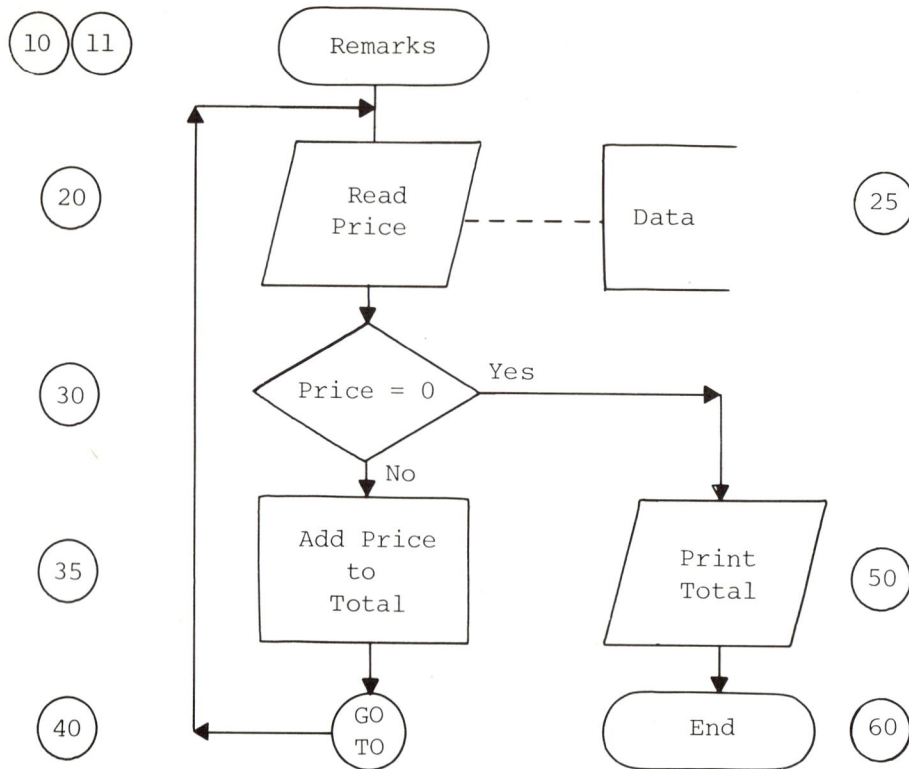

Figure 1-4

Program Flowchart—Grocery Check-out for One Customer

The "dummy" price in this problem is zero, an
impossible price in a grocery store today.  We
will use a "dummy" value in almost every program
we write and, in each case, we will choose a data
value that cannot possibly be correct in the
context of that problem.

Sometimes it is helpful to list the steps in sequence
before drawing the flowchart.  We can use a sequence
similar to that used in the check-out example:

a-  Input—enter the price of an item into the
    computer.  The READ statement will do this.

b-  Transfer—if there are no more items, skip or
    branch to Step 5.  The IF-THEN statement is the
    conditional transfer statement.

c-  <u>Process</u>—add that price to a total amount
    (accumulate a total).  The LET statement does
    all the arithmetic.

d-  <u>Transfer</u>—branch back to Step 1.  GO TO is the
    unconditional branch statement.

e-  <u>Output</u>—print the total amount owed.  The PRINT
    statement causes the needed output to be printed.

> Please notice that we have broken down the
> solution to this problem into several steps.
> Each step does only one thing, just like a
> computer.  This is called "thinking like a
> computer."

3-  Code the computer program.  Figure 1-5 is the BASIC
    program to solve the grocery store problem.  Notice
    that line 20 is the READ statement which causes
    input to occur.  Line 30 is an IF-THEN statement
    which causes the computer to branch to another point
    in the program <u>if</u> there are no more items to be
    added.  Line 35 is a LET statement for adding up the
    individual prices.  Line 40 is a GO TO statement
    which causes the computer to branch back to line 20,
    and line 50 is a PRINT statement which causes the
    output of the total owed.

```
10 REMARK  THIS PROGRAM CALCULATES THE TOTAL FOR ONE GROCERY CUSTOMER
11 REMARK  P = ITEM PRICE T = TOTAL
20 READ P
25 DATA 2.53, .35, 1.09, .73, .12, 4.59, 0
30 IF P = 0 THEN 50
35 LET T = T + P
40 GO TO 20
50 PRINT T
60 END
```

Figure 1-5

BASIC Program—Grocery Check-out for One Customer

> When using some computer systems, you must
> "clear" a CPU storage cell before you use it,
> just like an adding machine.  In this program,
> you can clear the "adding machine," T, by
> adding this BASIC statement:
>
>     15 LET T = 0
>
> We will discuss the LET statement later in this
> chapter.

4- Translate the BASIC code into computer-usable form.

5- Enter program into computer storage.  I suggest that you try out your computer by "running" the BASIC program shown in Figure 1-5.

6- Correct any programming errors.

7- Test solution with sample data.  Manually add up the prices in the DATA statement at line 25.  The total is 9.41.  If the computer does not write out 9.41, you have made some error in your program.

8- Run the program, using "real" data.  This is not realistic for this first example.


EXPLANATION OF BASIC STATEMENTS

In this section, each of the BASIC statements in Figure 1-5 will be explained.  Additional examples will be given to help you understand how that statement may be used in other BASIC programs.

The REMARK Statement

```
10  REMARK THIS PROGRAM CALCULATES THE TOTAL FOR ONE GROCERY CUSTOMER
11  REMARK P = ITEM PRICE T = TOTAL
20  . . .
```

You should use the REMARK statement to describe the purpose of the program, identify the variables, give the date written, name the author, etc.  It does not affect the program but is used to make the program more easily understood (documentation).

Line 10 describes the purpose of the program, and line
11 identifies the variables to be used in the program.
(Variables will be discussed in relation to the READ
statement.)   REMARK may be abbreviated to REM as in the
following example:

> 100   REM PROGRAM CODED BY I. FORKNER

This statement identifies the author of the program.
REMARK statements may be put anywhere in the program.  They
appear in the printout of the program but do not affect the
program execution in any way.

The general form of the REMARK statement is

1-  Line number        Must precede each BASIC statement.

2-  REMARK or REM       Key word which indicates that a
                        message is to follow.

3-  Message             Used for documentation purposes
                        only.  It has no effect on the
                        execution of the program.  REMARKS
                        may be placed anywhere in a program.

## The READ Statement

```
  .
11  . . .
20  READ P
25  . . .
  .
```

Remember, the READ statement is used to supply data to
the computer for processing.  In line 20, the READ causes
one data value to be stored in a CPU storage cell.  The
letter P after the key word READ is called a variable.
This variable tells the computer to store each price in a
storage cell called P.

You make up the variables you use in a program by
following the BASIC rule

> A simple variable must be made up of one
> letter or one letter and one digit, in
> that order.

Examples of valid BASIC variables are X, A1, B4, C, T, Q9,

and M7.  The following variables are invalid and would keep
the computer from running the program:

| Variable | Invalid Because |
|----------|-----------------|
| HW | Contains more than one letter |
| 2T | Digit appears first |
| V& | Contains a character other than a letter or digit |
| NUMBER | Contains more than one letter |
| X23 | Contains more than one digit |

You should make up variables so that they indicate the
kind of data to be stored at that address.  For example,
in this program, the variable P stands for item price.  In
a payroll program, the input may be an employee's number,
his pay rate, and the hours he worked.  An appropriate
READ statement in this payroll program would be

     22   READ N, R, H

In this READ statement, N refers to the employee number,
R the pay rate, and H the hours worked.  Notice that the
variables are separated by commas.

> In any one program, you must be sure that
> you do not use the same variable to represent
> different data elements.  For instance, you
> cannot use the variable N for employee number
> and the variable N for the number of hours
> worked.  Variables in a program must be unique.

In the grocery check-out program, the READ statement will
cause only one data value to be input each time the statement
is executed.  In the payroll example, three data values would
be stored in the CPU.

The general form of the READ statement is

1- Line number     Must precede each BASIC statement.

2- READ            Key word which causes the computer
                   to transfer data to CPU.

3- One or more     Identify CPU storage addresses in
   variables       which data will be stored.  Variables
                   must be made up of one letter or

one letter and one digit.  Variables
must be separated by commas.

Now It's Your Turn

1-  Correct any errors in the following statements:

       10   RIMARK THEIR MAY BE SOMETHIN WRONG WITH THESE STATEMENTS
       20   READ H, NUM, 3R, H

       10   _____
       20   _____
*****

       10   REMARK THERE MAY BE SOMETHING WRONG WITH THESE STATEMENTS
       20   READ H, N, R3, H1

The only necessary correction in line 10 is the correct
spelling of REMARK.  The other misspelled or incorrect words
will not make any difference in your program.  But you
should try to spell correctly.  In line 20, the variables
NUM and 3R are incorrect.  Remember, you may use only one
letter OR one letter and one digit, in that order.  Also,
you may not use a variable to represent more than one data
element.  The second H must be changed so that it is
unique.  You could have changed it as I did, or you could
have used a different letter.  And be sure you separate
these variables with commas.

2-  You are writing a program to prepare charge account
customer bills.  You want to enter data about each charge
sale that includes a customer number, a product identification number, the number of units purchased, and the
price of each unit.  Write a BASIC statement that will
cause the computer to enter these data.

_____
*****

I would write a READ statement as follows:

30  READ C, I, U, P

I hope you did not forget a line number.  Also, you should
have used <u>four</u> variables that give a clue to what they
represent.  I used C for <u>c</u>ustomer, I for <u>i</u>dentification,
U for <u>u</u>nits, and P for <u>p</u>rice.  You could have used W, X, Y,
and Z and be correct, but you could get in trouble later
in your program when you try to remember what variables
to use when you want to multiply the number of units times
the unit price.

<u>Back to the Sample Program—The DATA Statement</u>

```
     .
20   . . .
25   DATA 2.53, .35, 1.09, .73, .12, 4.59, 0
30   . . .
     .
```

The DATA statement at line 25 is one common method for
making data available to the program.  In this program, each
time the READ P statement is executed, one data element
from those listed in the DATA statement is stored in P.
For example, after the first execution of the READ P
statement CPU storage will be

(CPU address)

(Contents of storage)

P

2.53

After the second execution, CPU storage will be

P

.35

Each time a new data element is READ and stored in P, the
data stored first are erased and replaced with the new data.
When all data in the DATA statement have been READ, the
computer will loop back and try to READ another data value.
If there are no more data values, the computer will stop
after printing a NO DATA message.  In the grocery check-out
program, we must print the total amount owed after we have
finished READing all the data.  We can avoid the NO DATA
action by including a "dummy" data value.  This last data

value should not be a valid or possible data value in the
program.  In the check-out program, no item could have a
price of $0.00.  Therefore, the "0" data value in line 25
is used as the last or dummy data value.  Its use will be
explained when we discuss line 30.

Notice that the grocery prices are dollars and cents.
We must be sure to put in the decimal point in the data as
we did in line 25.  The commas in line 25 separate each
data value from the others.  When data values are very large
numbers, you must not use a comma to separate thousands
from hundreds.  For example, if a data value were 12,500,
the DATA statement should be written

    22  DATA 12500

Here is another example of READ and DATA statements.
If we want to process five employees in the payroll
program, we would write the following BASIC statements:

    22  READ N, R, H
    23  DATA 234556, 5.25, 43.1
    24  DATA 235663, 3.75, 38.5
    25  DATA 365479, 6.30, 41.0
    26  DATA 569872, 4.55, 37.3
    27  DATA 698342, 2.75, 45.8
    28  DATA 0, 0, 0

Each time this READ statement is executed, a different
set of data values are stored in the CPU as follows:

First Execution

| N | R | H |
|---|---|---|
| 234556 | 5.25 | 43.1 |

Second Execution

| N | R | H |
|---|---|---|
| 2345663 | 3.73 | 38.5 |

· · ·

Fifth Execution

| N | R | H |
|---|---|---|
| 698342 | 2.75 | 45.8 |

The general form of the DATA statement is

| | | |
|---|---|---|
| 1- | Line number | Must precede each BASIC statement. |
| 2- | DATA | Key word which causes the computer to save the data elements following DATA. |
| 3- | Data elements | May be either integer or decimal values.  Commas must be used to separate the data elements; therefore, commas may not be used to separate thousands from hundreds; i.e., 5,257 would not be allowed. Decimal values must include the decimal point. |
| | | Data elements may include a sign (+ or -) but may not include fractions (½ or 3 1/3). |

## READ/DATA Relationships

Several points are important to remember in relation to the READ/DATA statements:

1- Each time the READ statement is executed, new data are stored, and the old data are erased.

2- Data elements will be used from the DATA statement(s) in the same order as the left-to-right order of the variables following the READ statement.

3- The number of data elements used during each execution of the READ statement will be the same as the number of variables following the READ.

4- Unless the program provides for some method to "sense" the last data element, the program will attempt to continue to execute the READ. When there are no more data, the computer will stop and print END OF DATA.

1-  Correct any errors in the following statements:

        50   DATA 12345, 95¢ $1,250.33
        51   23456   .87   $2,332.00


_____

_____

\*\*\*\*\*

        50   DATA 12345, .95, 1250.33
        51   DATA 23456, .87, 2332.00

The cent and dollar signs used in line 50 are incorrect.
Also, you must put commas between data elements, but you may
not include commas within numbers as in 1,250.33.  Line 51
does not start with the key word DATA, and commas are left
out between the data elements.

2-  You want to calculate the average age of a group of
men and women students.  You need to cause the computer to
enter the data so that the average age of the men and the
average age of the women can be calculated.  We have decided
to designate men with a number 1 and women with a number 2.
The first five students are as follows:  woman, age 19;
man, age 22; man, age 18; woman, age 23; and man, age 20.
Write the BASIC statements that will cause these data to
be entered for processing.


        _____

        _____

        _____

        _____

        _____

\*\*\*\*\*

You should have written a READ statement and five DATA
statements, something like this:

```
20  READ S, A
21  DATA 2, 19
22  DATA 1, 22
23  DATA 1, 18
24  DATA 2, 23
25  DATA 1, 20
```

Of course, you could have used different variables in the
READ statement.  I used S for sex and A for age.  You also
could have reversed the order of the variables so that the
age value was read first and then the sex code.  But if you
reversed the variables, you would also have to reverse the
order of the data.  Right?

An easier and more efficient way to write these
statements is

```
20  READ S, A
21  DATA 2, 19, 1, 22, 1, 18, 2, 23, 1, 20
```

We can include more than one "set" of data in a single DATA
statement.  In this example, the computer will use the first
two data elements when READ is first executed, the second
two data elements when READ is executed the second time, etc.
But you must be careful not to extend your data beyond
column 72 on a punch card or space 72 on the terminal.

Back to the Sample Program—The IF-THEN Statement

```
    .
25  . . .
30  IF P = 0 THEN 50
35  . . .
    .
```

Line 30 is an example of the IF-THEN statement which
causes the computer to make a decision.  The computer will
change or not change the sequence of the program depending
on the results of the decision (conditional transfer).  In
this example, the computer compares the value stored in P
with a 0 (zero).  If P is equal to zero(=), the answer is
"yes."  The computer changes the sequence by branching to

the line number following THEN.  In this case, the computer
will branch to line 50 and execute the PRINT statement.

If, however, P is not equal to zero, the answer is "no."
The computer will not change the sequence and will continue
to line 35.

This statement is a typical example of using a "dummy"
data value to signal the end of data so that the program
may finish the problem as you wish.  The "zero" price
cannot be valid and is therefore used as a last data value.

In the sample program, after the first execution of
READ, P will hold a value of 2.53.  In the IF-THEN statement,
P will not equal zero.  The answer will be "no," and the
computer will continue to line 35.  As the program
continues, the values stored in P will cause the answer to
be "no" until the last data value, zero, is READ and stored
in P.  At that time, the decision in the IF-THEN statement
will be "yes," and the computer will branch to line 50 to
PRINT the total.

The general logic of the IF-THEN statement is shown in
the flowchart segment below:

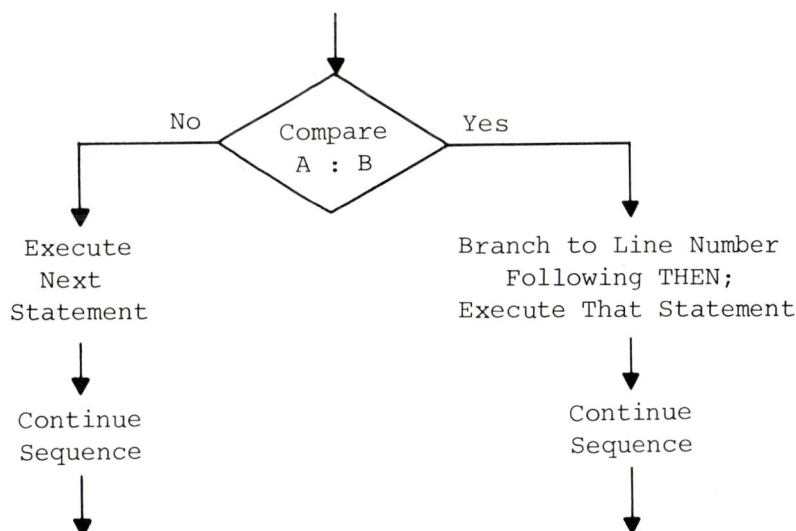

```
                          |
                          v
            No       / Compare \      Yes
         +----------<   A : B    >----------+
         |           \         /            |
         v                                  v
     Execute                      Branch to Line Number
      Next                          Following THEN;
    Statement                     Execute That Statement
         |                                  |
         v                                  v
     Continue                           Continue
     Sequence                           Sequence
         |                                  |
         v                                  v
```

This flowchart segment shows a decision symbol (diamond)
which represents the IF-THEN statement.  The two values
(A and B) are compared.  If the answer is "no," the program
continues to the next statement in sequence.  The program

then continues to execute each following statement in
sequence.

If the answer is "yes," the program branches to the
statement specified by the line number following THEN.
That statement is executed, and the program continues in
sequence from that point.

> Some computer systems use IF-GO TO rather
> than IF-THEN, while others allow you to use
> either form.  I suggest that you check with
> your instructor or your computer center to
> make sure you use a form that works on your
> computer.

## Other IF-THEN Decisions

Other decisions or comparisons that may be made in
BASIC and their symbols are

| | |
|---|---|
| Less than | A < B |
| Greater than | A > B |
| Less than or equal to | A <= B |
| Greater than or equal to | A >= B |
| Not equal to | A <> B |

The payroll problem will give us another example of the
IF-THEN statement.  Assume that employees working more than
40 hours per week are to receive overtime pay.  (Remember,
H is the storage address for hours worked.)  The flowchart
segment showing this decision is

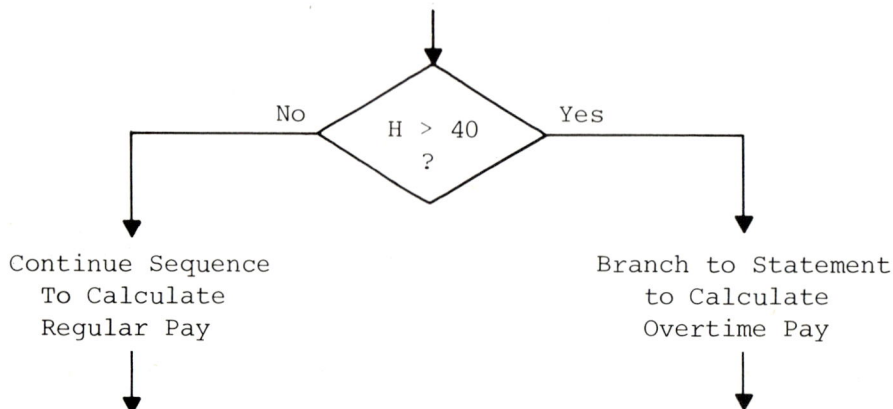

```
                              |
                              v
              No          / H > 40 \          Yes
        +---------------<  \   ?   / >---------------+
        |                   \    /                   |
        v                    \  /                    v
  Continue Sequence                           Branch to Statement
    To Calculate                                 to Calculate
    Regular Pay                                  Overtime Pay
        |                                            |
        v                                            v
```

The BASIC statement that will tell the computer to make this decision is

```
.
200  IF H > 40 THEN 450
250  . . . . .
```

If an employee worked more than 40 hours, the answer is "yes," and the program branches to line 450 to calculate overtime pay.  If he worked 40 or less hours, the answer is "no," and the program will continue to line 250 to calculate regular pay.

The general form of the IF-THEN statement is

| | | |
|---|---|---|
| 1- | Line number | Must precede each BASIC statement. |
| 2- | IF | Key word signaling a decision. |
| 3- | Decision | Between two variables or one variable and one constant.  These must be separated by one of the BASIC decision symbols. |
| 4- | THEN<br>GO TO | Key word indicating the line number to which the program should branch when the decision is "yes." |
| 5- | Line number | Point within the program to which the program will branch when the decision is "yes." |

Now It's Your Turn

1- Correct any errors you find in the following statement:

```
50  IF X EQUALS Y THEN 80
```

_____

\*\*\*\*\*

You can't use the word "equals" so your statement should look like this:

```
50  IF X = Y THEN 80
```

2- Correct any errors you find in the following statement:

```
60  IF 3 > 4 GO TO 20
```

_____

\*\*\*\*\*

There is not much point in comparing two constants.
This answer will always be "no."  You need to change one of
the constants into a variable like this:

    60   IF 3 > Q GO TO 20

The GO TO could be OK depending on your computer, and it is
correct to branch back toward the beginning of a program.
3- Remember the average age problem back on page 23?  We
wanted to calculate the average age for women students and
the average age for men students.  The data indicated the
sex with a 1 for men and a 2 for women.  Write a BASIC
statement that will tell the computer to decide whether or
not a person is a woman.

---

*****

    Here is what you should have written:

    80   IF S = 1 THEN 110

In this case, the men's calculations would be made at line
110, while the women's would have been made at line 81.

Back to the Sample Program—The LET Statement

    .
    30   . . .
    35   LET T = T + P
    40   . . .

    Line 35 is an example of a BASIC arithmetic statement.
The key word LET causes the computer to calculate the
value of the arithmetic expression to the right of the
equal sign.  The answer is then stored in the storage cell
named by the variable to the left of the equal sign.

> An expression may be a number (a constant), a
> variable, or a combination of constants and
> variables separated by arithmetic symbols.  An
> expression usually appears to the right of an
> equal sign.

    In the LET statement at line 35, the value stored in P

is added to the value stored in T.  The resulting answer
replaces the value previously stored in T.  After the first
execution of the READ statement, storage areas P and T will
contain

| P | T |
|---|---|
| 2.53 | 0 |

When you clear the "adding machine" with
LET T = 0 your computer erases any previously
stored value and puts a zero in that storage
cell.

The LET statement at line 35 will cause the computer to add
the values stored in P and T as follows:

$$
\begin{array}{r}
T = 0 \\
+P = \underline{2.53} \\
T = 2.53
\end{array}
$$

CPU storage after line 35 is executed will be

| P | T |
|---|---|
| 2.53 | 2.53 |

The second time the READ statement is executed, P and
T will contain

| P | T |
|---|---|
| .35 | 2.53 |

After the LET statement is executed, CPU storage will
be

| P | T |
|---|---|
| .35 | 2.88 |

After the final execution of the READ statement, P and
T will contain

| P | T |
|---|---|
| 0 | 9.41 |

> BASIC automatically keeps the decimal points
> properly lined up and places the decimal point
> correctly whenever multiplication and division
> are carried out.

## BASIC Arithmetic Operators

The arithmetic operators in BASIC and their meanings
are

| | |
|---|---|
| + | Addition |
| - | Subtraction |
| * | Multiplication |
| / | Division |
| ** or ↑ | Exponentiation (raise to a power; e.g., square a number) |

## Examples of BASIC Arithmetic Statements

A BASIC LET statement that will calculate the gross pay
for the second employee listed on page 21 is

```
112   LET G = H * R
```

We will have READ the data about this employee and stored
the hours worked in H and the pay rate in R.  The CPU
storage will look like this:

| N | R | H | G |
|---|---|---|---|
| 235663 | 3.75 | 38.5 | 234.41 |

The LET statement will cause the value stored in H to be
multiplied by the value stored in R.  The answer will then be
stored in G.

The LET statement will work like this:

```
112   LET G = H * R
      LET G = 38.5 * 3.75
      LET G = 144.37
```

After the LET statement is executed, CPU storage will look
like this:

| N | R | H | G |
|---|---|---|---|
| 235663 | 3.75 | 38.5 | 144.37 |

Notice that the contents of addresses N, R, and H did not
change but that the previous contents of address G were
erased and replaced with the gross pay for this employee.
Notice also that there is only one variable at the left of
the equal sign.

Here is another example of the LET statement.  Assume we
want to calculate the annual depreciation expense for a
delivery truck.  Depreciation expense = (new cost of truck -
trade-in value) ÷ years of useful life.  The LET statement
to make this calculation is

```
225  LET D = (C - T) / L
```

If the cost = $5000, the trade-in value = $1000, and the
useful life = 5 years, this LET statement will work as
follows:

```
225  LET D = (C - T) / L
     LET D = (5000 - 1000) / 5
     LET D = (4000) / 5
     LET D = 800
```

Notice the parentheses.  These cause the subtraction to
occur first; then the division occurs, giving us the
correct answer.

Perhaps another example will help you understand the LET
statement.  The area of a circle equals PI (3.1416) times the
radius squared.  In mathematical notation, $a = 3.1416r^2$.  The
LET statement to calculate the area of a circle is

```
330  LET A = 3.1416 * R ** 2
```

If the radius of a circle is 3 inches, this LET statement will
work like this:

```
330   LET A = 3.1416 * R ** 2
      LET A = 3.1416 * 3²
      LET A = 3.1416 * 9
      LET A = 28.2744
```

Notice that we had to include the times sign, *, between
3.1416 and r.  You must include all operators in a LET
statement.  You cannot assume or imply a multiplication
operation as you can in algebra.

Returning to the payroll problem, we see that the LET
statement to calculate the gross pay for an employee who
works more than 40 hours during the week is

```
212   LET G = R * 40 + (H - 40) * R * 1.5
```

This example shows multiplication, subtraction, and addition.
It also shows the use of parentheses which must be included in
this statement in order to calculate the correct gross pay.

If we had not used the parentheses, the computer would
have calculated 40 * R * 1.5 and subtracted that intermediate
answer from R * 40 + H, which would have been incorrect.
Parentheses are used to change the normal order in which
arithmetic operations are done.  The order is

First—exponentiation.

Second—multiplication and division, from left to right.

Third—addition and subtraction, from left to right.

Expressions enclosed in parentheses, if any, are done first,
using the order shown above.

Figure 1-6 shows the order your computer follows to make
the overtime gross pay calculations at line 212.

Notice that your computer does only one calculation at a
time.  The first calculation in Figure 1-6 is the subtraction

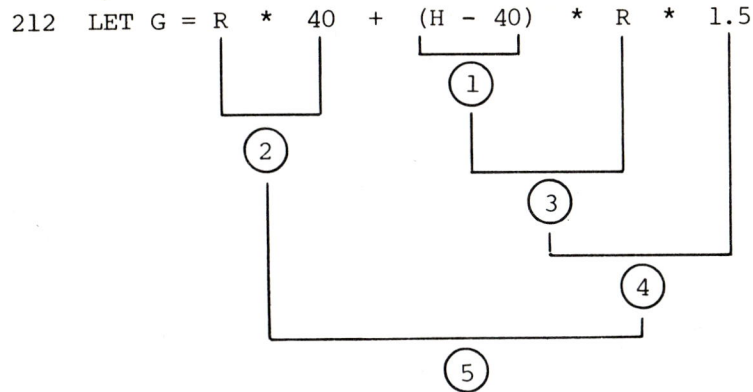

```
212  LET G = R  *  40  +  (H - 40)  *  R  *  1.5
```

Figure 1-6

Order of Execution—Overtime Gross Pay Calculation

of 40 from H—caused by the parentheses.  The numbers in the
small circles indicate the order of execution.

Figure 1-7 shows the order your computer follows to make
an _incorrect_ calculation of overtime gross pay.  Notice that
the parentheses are omitted and that the order of execution is
quite different.

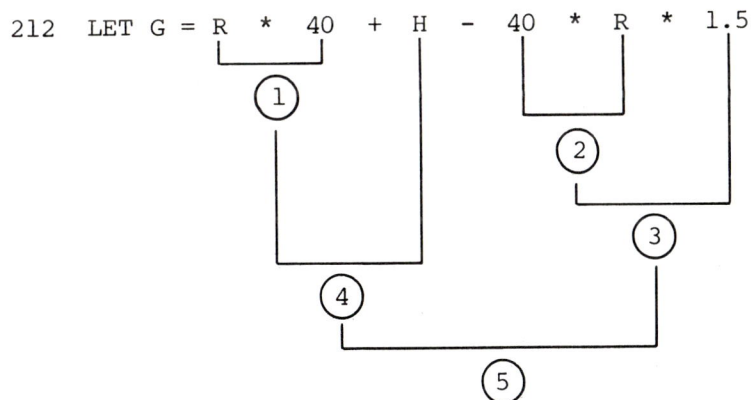

```
212  LET G = R  *  40  +  H  -  40  *  R  *  1.5
```

Figure 1-7

Order of Execution—Incorrect Overtime Gross Pay Calculation

Here are some simple algebra problems and a LET statement for each.  Study these carefully, and make sure you understand why the LET is coded as it is.

| | | |
|---|---|---|
| $x = 2y + 3z$ | 400 | LET X = 2 * Y + 3 * Z |
| $y = (a + b)^2$ | 401 | LET Y = (A + B) ** 2 |
| $h = \sqrt{a^2 + b^2}$ | 402 | LET H = (A ** 2 + B ** 2) ** .5 |
| $v = lwh$ | 403 | LET V = L * W * H |

The general form of the LET statement is

| | | |
|---|---|---|
| 1- | Line number | Must precede each BASIC statement. |
| 2- | LET | Key word causing an arithmetic operation. |
| 3- | Variable | May use only <u>one</u> variable to left of equal sign. |
| 4- | = | Must separate variable on its left from arithmetic expression on its right. |
| 5- | Expression | May be a numeric constant, a variable which holds a numeric value, or a combination of constants and variables separated by arithmetic operators. |
| 6- | Order of execution | First, expression within parentheses; second, exponentiation; third, multiplication and division; and fourth, addition and subtraction. |

## Now It's Your Turn

1-  Assume an employee worked 42 hours at $4.00 and that we pay time-and-a-half for overtime (hours worked more than 40). Calculate his gross pay using line 212 on page 32.

Gross pay = _____

*****

If you didn't get an answer of 172, review the order of execution above and try again.

2-  Now, calculate the employee's gross pay from Exercise 1 but omit the parentheses in your calculation.

Gross pay = _____

*****

```
   Gross pay = -38
```

How would you like to get a paycheck based on a minus $38
gross pay.

3-   Code a BASIC statement for each of the following arithmetic
formulas:

300    $x = \dfrac{a + b}{d - z}$   _____

301    $c = a + \dfrac{b}{d} - z$_____

302    $f = 2ab^2$   _____

303    $y = a^2 + 2ab + b^2$   _____

*****

```
   300  LET X = (A + B) / (D - Z)
   301  LET C = A + B / D - Z
   302  LET F = 2 * A * B ** 2
   303  LET Y = A ** 2 + 2 * A * B + B ** 2
```

Please notice that you __must__ separate all values in an
expression with one of the BASIC arithmetic operators at
lines 302 and 303.  Also, you must use parentheses in
line 300.  If you left out the parentheses, the computer
would solve the following:

$$x = a + \dfrac{b}{d} - z$$

This is certainly not the same problem as that shown in line
300 above.

Back to the Sample Program—The GO TO Statement

```
   .
35  . . .
40  GO TO 20
50  . . .
```

Line 40 is an example of an unconditional transfer statement.  Remember, the IF-THEN statement is a conditional
transfer statement.  The GO TO 20 causes the computer to
unconditionally transfer program control to line 20 and to

execute that statement and then to continue the program from that point.

You may use the GO TO statement to transfer control to any point in a program, either to a statement occurring before the GO TO as in this instance or to a point after the GO TO. You may use several GO TO statements in one program, all of which transfer the control to the same point or to several different points.

The general form of the GO TO statement is

1- Line number      Must precede all BASIC statements.

2- GO TO            Key words which signal an unconditional transfer.

3- Line number      Specifies the point in the program to which control is to be transferred.

The PRINT Statement

```
   .
40  . . .
50  PRINT T
60  . . .
```

Line 50 is an example of the output statement in BASIC. The key word PRINT causes the computer to display the output you want.  It is either printed or shown on a CRT (cathode ray tube) terminal.  This PRINT statement will cause the system to display the value stored in T, 9.41.

In BASIC, the computer automatically spaces the output line across the page, which is divided into five print zones of 15 spaces each.

Computer systems differ in this respect.  Some set up only 14 spaces, while others provide 18. Also, IBM's BASIC provides six print zones when the output is directed to a printer.

The PRINT statement at line 50 will cause only the first print zone to be used.  The numbers, 9.41, will be printed or shown at the left margin of the output line, as follows:

| 1 | 15 | 30 | 45 | Print Positions |
|---|----|----|----|-----------------|

9.41

In the payroll example discussed above, the PRINT statement that will cause the computer to write out the employee's number, his pay rate, the hours he worked, and his gross pay will be

    320  PRINT N, R, H, G

For the first employee, the output will appear as follows:

|     |      |      |        | Print Positions |
|-----|------|------|--------|-----------------|
| 1   | 15   | 30   | 45     |                 |
| 234556 | 5.25 | 43.1 | 234.41 |                 |

The output is automatically spaced across the page.  Each value is printed in a 15-space print zone in the same order as the variables listed after the PRINT statement.  You may change the output line in several ways.  These will be discussed in later chapters.

The general form of the PRINT statement is

| | | |
|---|---|---|
| 1- | Line number | Must precede each BASIC statement. |
| 2- | PRINT | Key word which activates the output device. |
| 3- | Headings, messages, blanks, constants, and/or variable names | Specifies what the computer is to print. |

Now It's Your Turn

1-  Remember the average age problem on page 23?  You could have calculated the average age of the men and stored the answer in A1 and that of the women in A2.  Write a BASIC statement that will output those two answers.

_____

*****

    120  PRINT A1, A2

In this statement, you tell the computer to print out the values stored in A1 and A2, respectively.  Simple, isn't it?

2-  In the sample problem, you want to tell the computer to output each price just after it is READ.  Write a BASIC statement that will do that.  Refer to Figure 1-5, page 15.

_____

*****

```
21  PRINT P
```

Notice that the READ statement is numbered 20 and that a
value is stored in P.  Your PRINT statement should therefore
be numbered 21 and should tell the computer to PRINT the
value stored in P.

### Back to the Sample Program—The END Statement

```
   .
50  . . .
60  END
```

Line 60 signals to the computer that the program is
completed.  The END statement must be the last statement in
a BASIC program.  Therefore, END must have the highest line
number in the program.

The general form of the END statement is

1-  Line number      Must be the highest line number in
                     the program.

2-  END              Key word signals the end of the program.

### NOW IT'S YOUR TURN PROBLEM—PAYROLL CONTROL

In this exercise, we are going to go through a
complete program one step at a time.  Hopefully,
this will give you an overview of the program
writing process and provide a model that you can
use to write other BASIC programs.

The problem we are going to solve is a management control
program to ensure the accuracy of our payrolls.  We are going
to calculate, in this program, the gross pay for all hourly
paid employees and accumulate those amounts to provide a total.
We will then accumulate all gross pay amounts in our regular
payroll "run" and compare the two totals.  If the totals agree,
we can assume our actual payroll is correct.  If the totals
are not equal, we will need to make some corrections.

Our output from the payroll control program will be one
grand total of all the individual gross pay amounts.  The only

input we need is the hours worked by each employee and his pay
rate.  We must make three calculations (processes):  (1) regular
time gross pay, (2) overtime gross pay, and (3) accumulate the
grand total.  And we should be able to do this job with only
two conditional transfers:  last data and hours worked
compared to 40.

Figure 1-8 is the program flowchart that gives you one
planned solution to this problem.  The numbers in the small
circles are included to give us common line numbers with which
to work.

You should try to fill out each space before looking at
my suggested answer.  Refer to the section of the chapter that
presented that kind of BASIC statement.  Take your time.

Line 10:  Your first BASIC statement should identify the problem
and the programmer.

10 _____

*****

Your line 10 should have started with REM or REMARK, like
this:

    10  REM PAYROLL CONTROL PROGRAM   ANDERSON

Remember, REMARK statements do not affect your program.  But
you should use REMARKs to document your program.

Line 15:  According to the program flowchart, your next
statement is supposed to enter two data elements for one
employee, his hours worked and his pay rate.

15 _____

*****

Your statement should look like this:

    15  READ H, R

If you want to enter two data elements, you should list two
variables after READ.  The variables you use could be different
from these, but using names that give a clue helps you to keep
track of what is happening in your program.

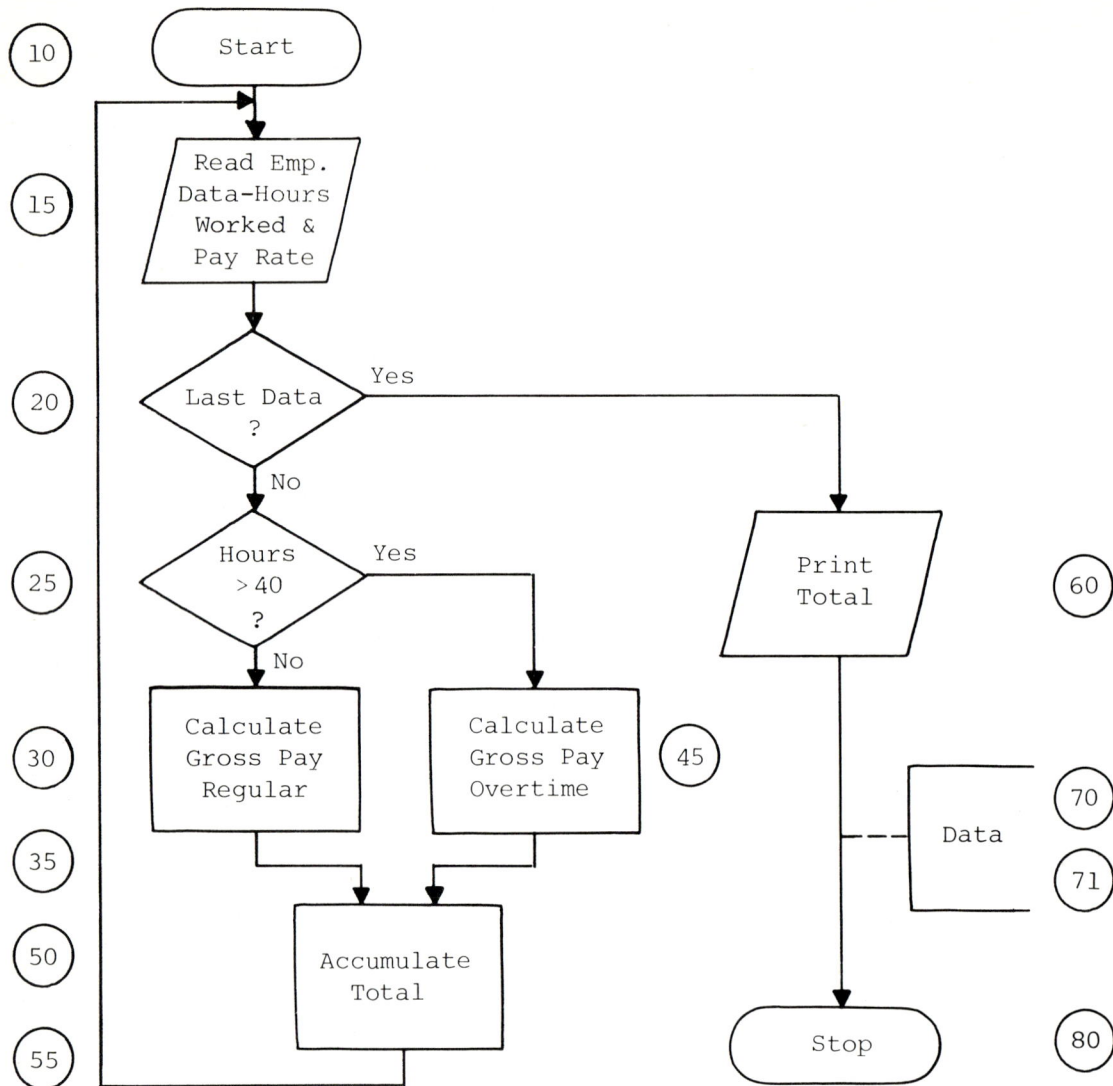

Figure 1-8

Program Flowchart—Payroll Control

Line 20:  This line should test for the end of data.  You
should be careful to select a data value that is impossible
in the context of this problem.  For example, a pay rate of
zero dollars is impossible, but zero hours worked is possible.
The employee may be on vacation.

20 _____

*****

I hope you started this statement with IF, as follows:

    20  IF R = 0 THEN 60

Any time you want to test or compare or decide, you use the IF
statement followed by a comparison of two values.  In this
statement, we are comparing the current value stored in R with
0.  If they are equal, the program branches to line 60.  If the
two values are not equal, the program continues to the next
line in sequence.

Line 25:  Here is another decision.  With this one, you want
to tell the computer to decide whether or not an employee
worked more than 40 hours.

    25_____

*****

    Remember that "equal to" is not the only possible comparison.

    25  IF H > 40 THEN 45

Notice that the "yes" branch in the flowchart points to the
symbol numbered 45 where you will calculate the gross pay for
overtime.

Line 30:  You are supposed to calculate the gross pay for
employees who worked 40 or less hours.  Remember that * means
multiplication.

    30_____

*****

    This should have been an easy one for you.  You want to
multiply the hours worked by the pay rate and save the answer
like this:

    30  LET G = H * R

If you used a place other than G to store your gross pay, that's
OK.  But you cannot put the H * R to the left of the equal sign.

Line 35:  If you don't put this line in your program, your
answer will be wrong.  You need to be careful at this point
in your program to be sure that the sequence you program will
produce the correct answer.  You will notice that the arrow
in the flowchart from the process at 30 points directly to
the process at 50.  This is a very easy statement to write,
but it is extremely important in this program.

    35 _____
*****

    Your line 35 should look like this:

    35  GO TO 50

If you omitted this statement, your program would compute the
gross pay at line 30 and then would continue to line 45 to
calculate the gross pay again.  The second time would have
been incorrect.

Line 45:  This statement should calculate the gross pay for
employees who worked more than 40 hours during the week.  There
are several ways we can make this calculation, but remember that
the employee is to receive one and one-half times his pay rate
for each hour he worked over 40.

    40 _____
*****

    If you have a good memory, you will recall that on page 32
this statement was done for you.

    45  LET G = R * 40 + (H - 40) * R * 1.5

If you missed this one, I suggest that you refer to the
discussion on pages 32 and 33.

Line 50:  The program flowchart shows that you are to write
a statement to accumulate the gross pay for all employees.
This accumulation is very similar to the accumulation of the
prices in the grocery check-out example.

    50 _____

*****

     50  LET T = T + G

You should have noticed now that anytime you want to
accumulate values, you will use the same variable on both
sides of the equal sign.  In this example, I used T = T.
This kind of calculation is very common in business applications, and you should make sure that you understand how it
works.

Line 55:  The flowchart shows an arrow returning to the READ
statement.  This is another easy one.

    55 _____

*****

    You should have written an unconditional branch statement
to return the program to line 15:

    55  GO TO 15

Line 60:  This is the line to which we transferred when the
"yes" answer occurred at the last data decision.  The program
flowchart shows that you should tell the computer to display
the total.

    60 _____

*****

This statement is just like the one in the grocery check-out problem:

```
60  Print T
```

Remember, you want to tell the computer to display the value of your accumulation at line 45.

Lines 70, 71: Assume we have the following data about several employees:

| Hours Worked | Pay Rate |
|---|---|
| 38.0 | 3.00 |
| 44.4 | 3.50 |
| 39.9 | 2.80 |
| 41.2 | 3.40 |
| 40.0 | 4.00 |

70 _____

71 _____

*****

```
70  DATA  38.0, 3.00, 44.4, 3.50, 39.9, 2.80
71  DATA  41.2, 3.40, 40.0, 4.00, 0, 0
```

There are several things you should look at in your answer. Did you use commas to separate the data elements? Did you include the decimal points? And, very important, did you include the zero data values at the end of your data? Notice that you must include a "dummy" data value for each variable in your READ statement, two in this example. If you had only one zero, your computer would have tried to read two values, would have found only one, and would have stopped after printing OUT OF DATA AT 15.

Also, notice that in this program we put the DATA at the end of the program, But in the grocery check-out example, the DATA was placed immediately after the READ. Either placement will work. In fact, you may place the DATA anywhere in your program as long as the line numbers are in correct sequence and the DATA is before the END statement.

<u>Line 80</u>:  This is "the end."  Is that enough of a hint?

    80 _____

*****

The last statement in a BASIC program must be

80  END

Your completed BASIC program should look like that shown
in Figure 1-9.

```
10   REM PAYROLL CONTROL PROGRAM  ANDERSON
15   READ H, R
20   IF R = 0 THEN 60
25   IF H > 40 THEN 45
30   LET G = H * R
35   GO TO 50
45   LET G = R * 40 + (H - 40) * R * 1.5
50   LET T = T + G
55   GO TO 15
60   PRINT T
70   DATA 38.0, 3.00, 44.4, 3.50, 39.9, 2.80
71   DATA 41.2, 3.40, 40.0, 4.00, 0, 0
80   END
```

Figure 1-9

Now It's Your Turn Problem—Payroll Control


SUMMARY

In this chapter we have presented the programming concept
of sequence, which indicates when an instruction will be
carried out.  Two coding rules were given:  Each statement
must be preceded by a line number, and a statement may not
exceed 72 spaces.  The main components of a computer program
are input, transfer, process, and output.  Most programs
include at least one loop which causes several statements to
be repeated.

Eight programming steps were given:  (1) study the
problem, (2) plan a solution, (3) code the computer program,
(4) translate the BASIC program into computer-usable form,
(5) enter the program into computer storage, (6) correct any

programming errors, (7) test the solution with sample data,
and (8) run the program.

The BASIC statements that have been presented in this
chapter and a summary of their general form are presented
below:

1- REMARK or REM      Used for documentation purposes
                      only; has no effect on the program.

line number  REMARK or REM  any desired message

2- READ               Major input statement.  Activates
                      input device and names CPU storage
                      areas in which data will be stored.

line number  READ  one or more variables

3- DATA               Provides numeric data values for
                      use in program.  Must be used with
                      READ statement.

line number  DATA  one or more numeric data values

4- IF-THEN            Conditional branch command.  Causes
   IF-GO TO           computer to branch to a different
                      point in program or to continue in
                      sequence, depending on condition of
                      comparison.

line number  IF  comparison  THEN  line number
                             GO TO

5- LET                Arithmetic statement, often referred
                      to as a replacement statement.  Causes
                      computer to calculate value of
                      expression and to store answer in
                      variable to left of equal sign.

line number  LET  variable = arithmetic expression

6- GO TO              Unconditional transfer command.
                      Causes computer to transfer control
                      to a different point in the program
                      specified by line number following
                      GO TO.

line number  GO TO  line number

7- PRINT              Output statement.  Causes computer
                      to print or display desired message,
                      headings, contents of CPU storage
                      area specified by variable name.

line number  PRINT  message, headings, variable(s)

8- END                Signals end of program.  Must be last
                      statement in BASIC program and must
                      have the highest line number.

highest line number  END

EXERCISES

A-  Write a BASIC statement for each of the following
arithmetic formulas:

1-  $n = \dfrac{x + y}{a3}$          2-  $i = p(1 + r)^n$

3-  $q = 3(5k^3 - 2)$          4-  $y = -i + jk^2$

B-  Write a BASIC statement that will cause the computer to
read and store each of the following:

1-  Sex code and age          2-  Age and income

3-  Credit rating, amount     4-  Employee number, number
    due, and age of the           of dependents, pay rate,
    account                       hours worked, and tax
                                  rate

C-  Make up some test data for each of the parts of Exercise
B, and code the BASIC statements necessary to provide these
data to the computer:

1-  Sex code:  1 = women, 2 = men.  (Exercise B-1)

2-  Credit rating:  1 = excellent, 2 = good, and 3 = poor.
    Age of Account:  30, 60, 90 days.  (Exercise B-3)

3-  Tax rates:  10%, 15%, or 20%.  (Exercise B-4)

D-  Write the BASIC statements that will cause the computer
to

1-  Select the women students as specified in Exercises
    B-1 and C-1.

2-  Select those who have worked overtime in Exercise B-4
    (worked more than 40 hours per week).

3-  Separate those with the three different credit ratings
    in Exercises B-3 and C-2.

4-  Separate employees according to tax rate in Exercises
    B-4 and C-3.

E-  Write the BASIC statement(s) that will cause the computer
to output

1-  The values stored for credit rating, amount due, and
    age of the account as specified in Exercise B-3.

2-  The values stored for employee number, gross pay,
    income tax, and net pay as specified in Exercise B-4.

F-  Make any required corrections in the following stand-alone
BASIC statements.  Do not make unneeded corrections.

    1-   READ A, 2.37, 4B, NUM
    2-   27 READ Z9, X, ZN .
    3-   30 GO TO 30
    4-   32 LET XY = 4.32 - X (X / Z)
    5-   41 GO TO 97346
    6-   43 IF A GREATER THAN B GO TO 30
    7-   IF Z = 3.17 THEN GO TO 500
    8-   60 LET C = A * C / D * 2)
    9-   75 PRINT A, B, C, D


PROBLEMS

1-  Code a BASIC program that will print an invoice (bill)
for one customer.  The bill will be sent to the customer and
will show the total amount he owes us for charge account
purchases.  Follow the flowchart shown in Figure 1-10.

| | |
|---|---|
| Output | One detail line for each item purchased:<br>    Item identification number (ID number)<br>    Quantity purchased (number of units)<br>    Price per unit<br>    Amount owed for that item<br><br>One summary line:<br>    Total amount owed |
| Input | One record for each item purchased:<br>    Item ID number<br>    Quantity purchased<br>    Price per unit |
| Process | 1-  Amount owed = quantity purchased x price per unit.<br>2-  Accumulate total of amount owed for all items<br>        purchased. |
| Transfer | Last item? |
| Test data | 912, 10, 22.50<br>194, 20, 14.25<br>481, 30, 1.27<br>234, 75, 5.50<br>0, 0, 0 |

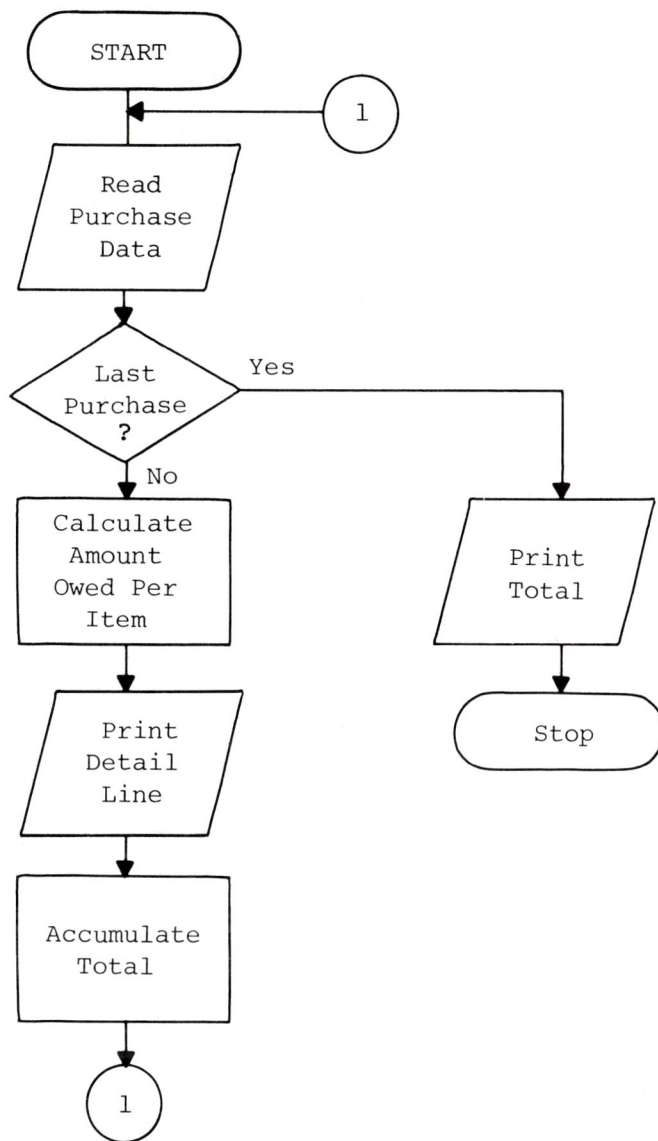

Figure 1-10

Flowchart—Problem 1

2-   Draw a flowchart; then write a BASIC program that will
print a purchase discount report showing the customer's number,
the total amount of the purchase, the amount of the discount,
and the net amount of the purchase.

| Amount of Purchase | Discount Percent |
|---|---|
| $100 or less | 0% |
| $101 to $300 | 1.5% |
| More than $300 | 3% |

Output
    One detail line for each purchase:
       Customer number
       Amount of purchase
       Amount of discount
       Net amount of purchase

    One summary line:
       Total purchase amounts
       Total discount amounts
       Total net amounts

Input
    One record for each purchase:
       Customer number
       Amount of purchase

Process
    Amount of discount = amount of purchase x discount
      percent.
    Net amount of purchase = amount of purchase - amount
      of discount.
    Accumulate totals.

Transfer
    Last purchase?
    Discount percent?

Test data
    426, 550
    381, 90
    230, 100
    580, 300
    221, 195
    0, 0

3-  Code a BASIC program that will prepare an accounts
receivable report.  Follow the flowchart shown in
Figure 1-11.

Output          One detail line for each customer:
                    Customer number
                    Balance due

Input           One master record for each customer:
                    Record code—0 = master record
                    Customer number
                    Previous balance due

                One or more transaction records for each customer:
                    Record code—1 = purchase, 2 = payment
                    Customer number
                    Amount of each transaction

                All records for one customer are grouped.  The first
                    record of each group will be a master record.

Process         Add purchase amounts.
                Subtract payments.
                Save customer master record.

Transfer        Last customer?
                Purchase?
                Payment?
                Different customer (new master record)?

Test data       0, 111, 100.50
                1, 111, 100.50
                2, 111, 100.50
                1, 111, 10.00
                0, 122, 0
                1, 122, 25.60
                1, 122, 3.40
                0, 133, 24.00
                2, 133, 24.00
                0, 144, 201.00
                1, 144, 10.50
                1, 144, 9.50
                0, 0, 0

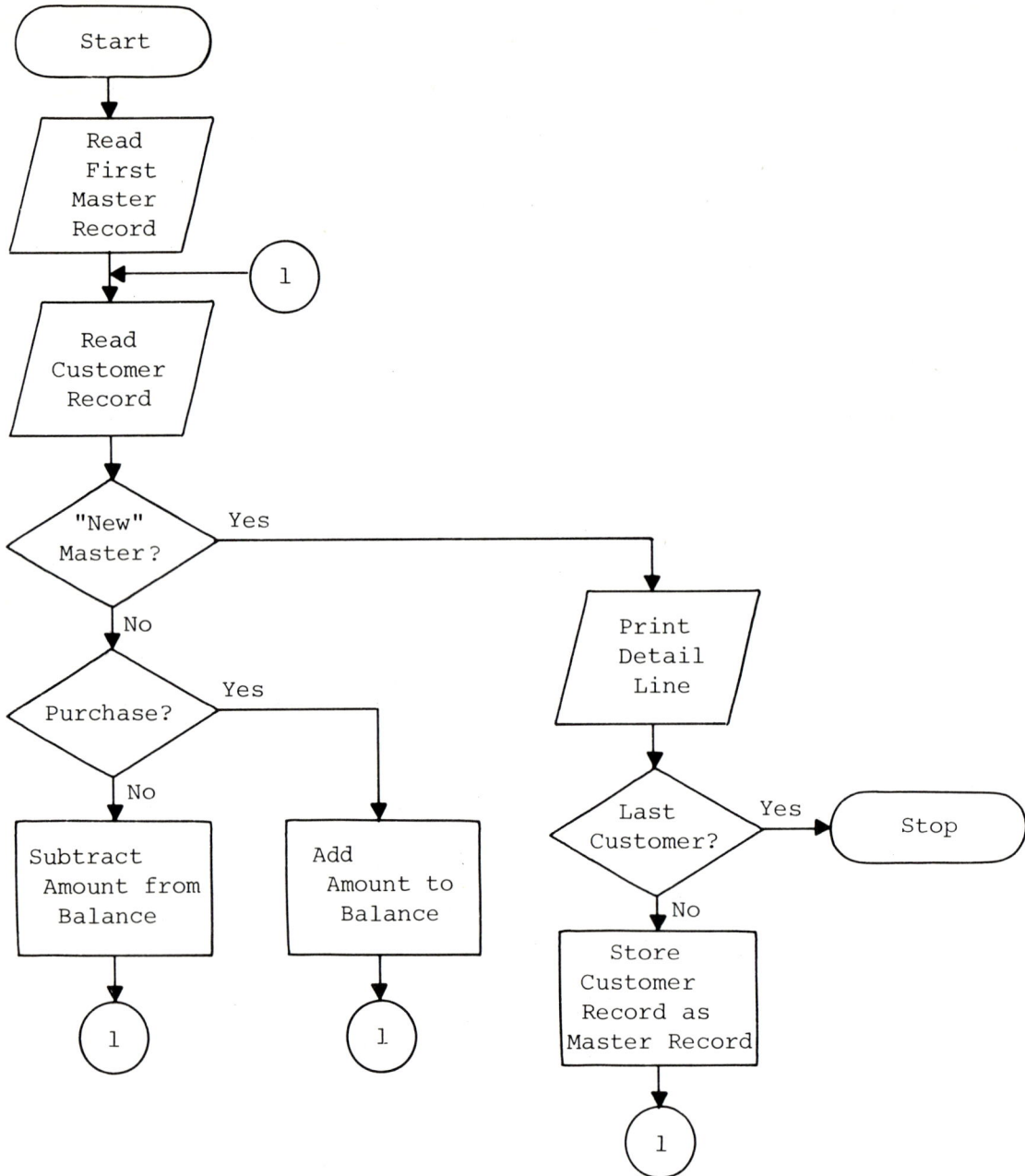

Figure 1-11
Flowchart—Problem 3

4-  Draw a flowchart and code a BASIC program to prepare a
monthly salesman's commission report.  The commission is 10%
of a salesman's total sales for the month.  We also have an
incentive program as follows:

| Total Sales | Bonus |
|---|---|
| More than $20,000 | 5% of total sales |
| $10,000 to $20,000 | 2% of total sales |
| Less than $10,000 | no bonus |

Output     One detail line for each salesman:
    Salesman number
    Total sales
    Commission
    Bonus (if any)
    Total commission

     One summary line:
    Accumulated total sales
    Accumulated commissions
    Accumulated bonus
    Accumulated total commissions

Input     One transaction record for each sale:
    Salesman number
    Total sales for month

Process     Calculate commission.
    Calculate bonus (if any).
    Calculate total commission (commission + bonus).
    Accumulate totals for sales, commissions, bonus,
      total commissions.

Transfer     Last salesman?
    Sales greater than 20000?
    Sales less than 10000?

Test data     123, 18000
    125, 8000
    224, 24000
    238, 20000
    255, 10000
    300, 22000
    231, 9500
    442, 16000
    550, 0
    0, 0

# 2

# More BASIC

## INTRODUCTION

In Chapter 1, you learned enough about BASIC programming so
that you could write and run simple business programs.  After
you have completed this chapter, you will be able to

1- Cause your computer to print good-looking business
   reports with appropriate titles and column headings.
2- Space your output across the page as you wish.
3- Space your output vertically.
4- Include dollar signs and limit the number of digits
   printed to the right of the decimal points.
5- Cause the computer to make multiple decisions with
   only one BASIC statement.

But first, some programming hints.

## PROGRAMMING CONCEPTS

Beginning programmers often have difficulty causing the
computer to print headings properly.  Another problem is
making sure the program sequence will calculate correct answers.
Hopefully, the following discussion will help you avoid these
two problems.

### Printing Headings

Most business reports require three types of output:
headings, detail lines, and one or more summary lines.  The
heading usually includes the report name or title.  Subheadings

are often used to identify the data included in each column.
These subheadings are usually called column headings.

Detail lines are the body of the report.  There is
usually one detail line for each item in the report, such as
an employee, a customer, or an item in inventory.  A summary
line is usually placed at the end of a report and provides
some kind of summary data to make the report more understandable.

A payroll register report with a title, column headings,
several detail lines, and a summary line are shown in Figure 2-1.

PAYROLL REGISTER

| NAME | GROSS PAY | INCOME TAX | NET PAY |
|------|-----------|------------|---------|
| John Adams | $351.25 | $70.04 | $281.21 |
| Bill Smith | $256.25 | $51.25 | $205.00 |
| Mary Wills | $283.50 | $56.60 | $226.90 |
| . | . | . | . |
| . | . | . | . |
| . | . | . | . |
| TOTAL | $2538.25 | $507.60 | $2030.65 |

Figure 2-1

Business Report with Headings, Detail, and Summary Lines

Notice that the report title is centered across the print
line and that each column is identified with a subheading.
This report segment shows three detail lines, one for each of
three employees.  The dots under the detail lines mean that
the rest of the detail lines have been omitted.  The report
ends with a summary line showing the total for each of the
amount columns.  I am sure you will agree that this report
is neat, is easy to read, and will give management the information it wants.

However, many beginning programmers make the mistake of

causing the title and column headings to be printed before
each detail line as follows:

PAYROLL REGISTER

| NAME | GROSS PAY | INCOME TAX | NET PAY |
|------|-----------|------------|---------|
| John Adams | $351.25 | $70.04 | $281.21 |

PAYROLL REGISTER

| NAME | GROSS PAY | INCOME TAX | NET PAY |
|------|-----------|------------|---------|
| Bill Smith | $256.25 | $51.25 | $205.00 |

PAYROLL REGISTER

This output does not look the way it should.  It is
difficult to read and will probably make any manager unhappy.
Figure 2-2 is a flowchart segment showing the program sequence
that causes this incorrect output.

You should notice that the "print title, column heads"

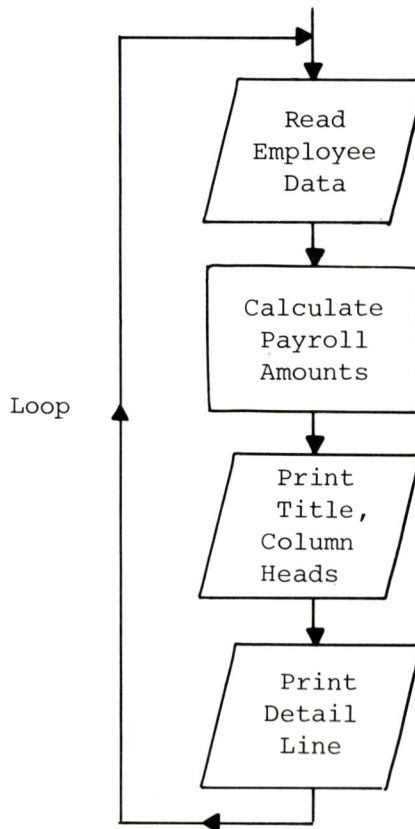

Figure 2-2

Flowchart—Heading Within Loop

symbol is placed within the program loop.  This will cause
the report title and the column headings to be printed just
before the detail line for each employee.

If you want to make the title and column headings print
only at the top of the report as in Figure 2-1, the "print
title, column heads" symbol should be placed outside the loop,
as shown in Figure 2-3.

If you want to print a summary line for the PAYROLL
REGISTER, you must put the appropriate PRINT statement after
the program loop.

Correct Program Sequence

Another frequent problem for beginning programmers is to
make sure the program calculates the correct answers.  It is
very frustrating to write a program, have it run without any

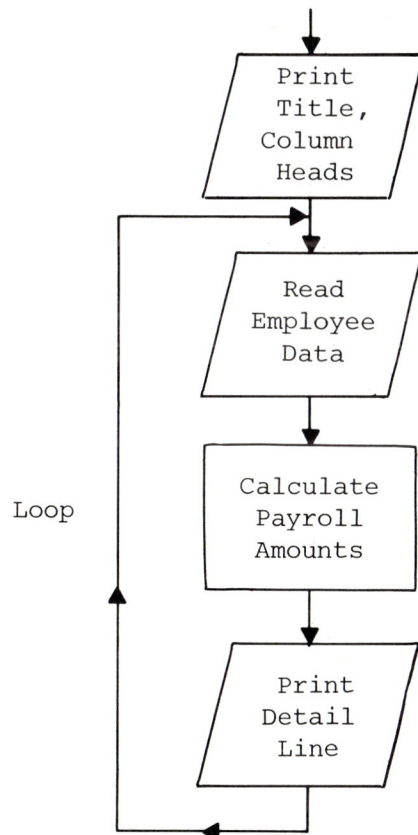

Figure 2-3

Flowchart—Heading Before Loop

error messages, and when you test your answer find it to be
incorrect.

To illustrate incorrect program logic (sequence) and how
it can be corrected, assume you are to prepare a sales
commission report.  The input consists of the salesman's
number and the amount of the sale.  If the amount of the sale
is more than $1000, the commission is equal to 10% of the
amount of the sale.  If the sale is equal to or less than
$1000, the commission is 6% of the sale.  The output detail
line will include the salesman's number, the amount of the
sale, and the amount of the commission.

Figure 2-4 is a program flowchart segment showing the
input, transfer, processes, and output to solve this problem.

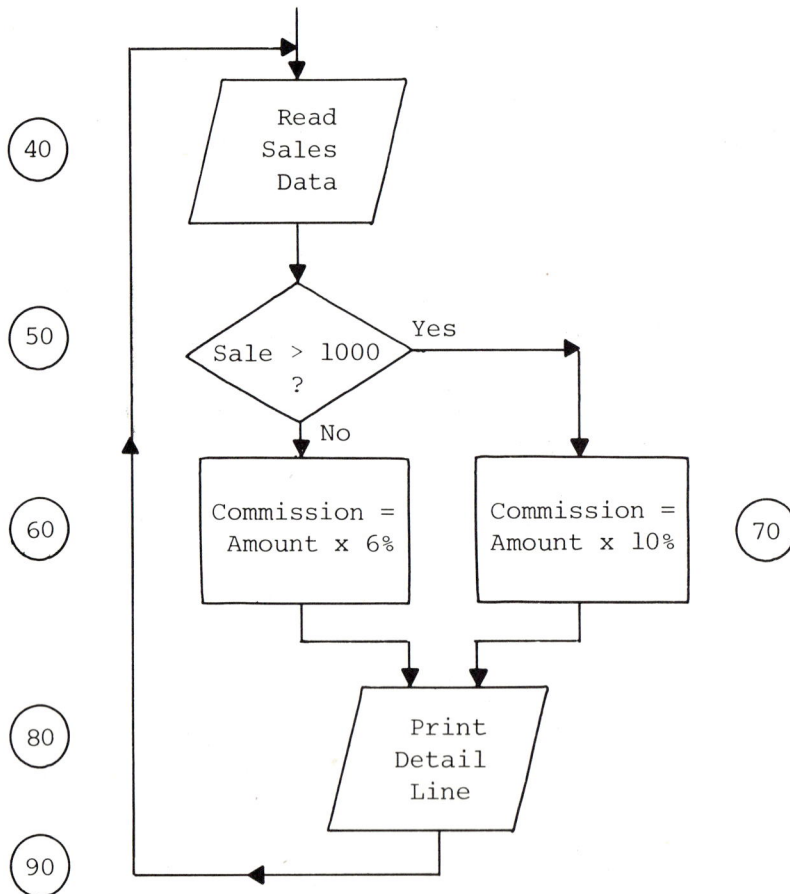

Figure 2-4

Program Flowchart—Sales Commissions

As a programmer, you could write the following BASIC
statements from the flowchart segment in Figure 2-4:

```
    .
40   READ N, A
50   IF A > 1000 THEN 70
60   LET C = A * .06
70   LET C = A * .10
80   PRINT N, A, C
90   GO TO 40
    .
    .
```

At first glance, this program segment appears to be
correct.  And the salesmen will really appreciate your
programming "skill."  But what happens when salesman #348
makes a sale of $800?

1- The answer to the question at line 50 is "no."

2- The computer continues to line 60 and calculates
   C = 800 * .06 = $48.

3- The computer then continues in sequence to line 70
   and calculates the commission again:
   C = 800 * .10 = $80.

4- The computer goes on to line 80 and prints the
   _incorrect_ commission amount.  (No wonder the salesman
   think you are Mr. Wonderful!)

If you write a program like this, all commissions will be
calculated at the 10% rate.  And that is not what the problem
requires.  Examine the flowchart in Figure 2-4 carefully.  You
should notice that the flow arrow goes directly from the "6%
commission" symbol to the "print detail" symbol.  Therefore
you must write your program so that this sequence will occur.
To do this, add a GO TO statement between lines 60 and 70, as
follows:

```
    .
60   LET C = A * .06
65   GO TO 80
70   LET C = A * .10
80   PRINT N, A, C
    .
```

Now the commission for salesman #348 will be calculated at line 60.  The GO TO statement will cause the computer to skip line 70 and go directly to line 80 to print out the correct commission, $48.00.

> If you wish to avoid this kind of error, you need to think like a computer.  Perhaps thinking through the steps of a program as shown above will help.

Now It's Your Turn

1-  The following program segment is supposed to print a report title, several detail lines, and a summary line.  If the resulting report will be unacceptable to management, correct it.

```
10   READ C, B
15   IF C = 0 THEN 50
20   LET A = C + B
25   LET T = T + A            (accumulates total)
30   PRINT "CUSTOMER REPORT"  (report title)
40   PRINT C, B, A            (detail line)
50   PRINT "TOTAL", T         (summary line)
60   GO TO 10
 .
 .
```

_____

_____

_____

_____

_____

_____

*****

This program segment will print the report heading, detail line, and a summary line for each transaction.  Not correct. The statements should be rearranged like this:

```
  5   PRINT "CUSTOMER REPORT"
 10   READ C, B
 15   IF C = 0 THEN 100
 20   LET A = C + B
 25   LET T = T + A
 40   PRINT C, B, A
 60   GO TO 10
  .   . . .
100   PRINT "TOTAL", T
```

Notice that the READ and LET statements are within the program loop.  These are used to create the values for the detail line, which is also included in the program loop.  But the report title is printed at the beginning of the program, and the summary line is printed at the end of the program, both outside the program loop.  (I sure hope you can find the program loop in this example.)

2-  Here is a program segment used by THE Electric Co. to bill its customers.  The electric rates are

    5 cents per kilowatt-hour (kWh) for 0-100 kilowatts (kW).
    $5 plus 3 cents per kWh for 101-200 kW.
    $8 plus 2 cents per kWh for all kW over 200.

We will enter the customer number and the kilowatt-hours used, calculate a bill for each customer, and print out the customer number, the kilowatt-hours used, and the amount of the bill.

```
    .
10   READ N, K
20   IF K <= 100 THEN 50
30   IF K <= 200 THEN 60
40   IF K > 200 THEN 70
50   LET B = .05 * K
60   LET B = 5 + .03 * (K - 100)
70   LET B = 8 + .02 * (K - 200)
80   PRINT N, K, B
    .
```

If you think there are any errors, correct them.

_____

_____

*****

    If you didn't make any corrections, you will have many unhappy customers.  You should have added the following statements to the program segment:

```
50   . . .
55   GO TO 80
60   . . .
65   GO TO 80
70   . . .
80   PRINT N, K, B
```

Can you explain why you must include these GO TO statements?

SAMPLE PROBLEM

This problem is another payroll problem but with a
different twist.  We are going to prepare a business report
showing the gross pay for each employee.  We should follow
the programming steps discussed in Chapter 1.

1- Study the problem.  This business report should
   include column headings and one detail line for each
   employee, including his name and the gross pay
   earned.  We will also print a summary line giving
   the total of all gross pay amounts with an
   appropriate message.
   We will need to enter the employee's name, shift
   code, hours worked, and pay rate.  The shift codes
   and their meanings are shown below:

| Shift | Times | Code | Bonus |
|-------|-------|------|-------|
| Day | 8:00 a.m. to 4:00 p.m. | 1 | 0 |
| Swing | 4:00 p.m. to 12:00 midnight | 2 | 10% |
| Graveyard | 12:00 midnight to 8:00 a.m. | 3 | 20% |

   Several processes are required to calculate gross pay
   depending on the different shifts worked and to
   accumulate all gross pay amounts.  Two conditional
   transfers will be used, one to test for last data and
   one to decide on the shift worked.  Several unconditional
   transfers must be used to assure correct program
   sequence, and one must be used to close the loop so
   that all employee records will be processed.

2- Plan a solution.  Figure 2-5 is a program flowchart
   showing the sequence of steps needed to produce this
   report.  Please pay close attention to the program
   sequence; the GO TO statements are not shown.

3- Code the computer program.  Figure 2-6 is the BASIC
   program to produce this business report.  Notice that
   new PRINT statements are used at lines 15, 400, 505,
   and 510.  Also, the first variable in the READ
   statement at line 20 is different so that the alphabetic

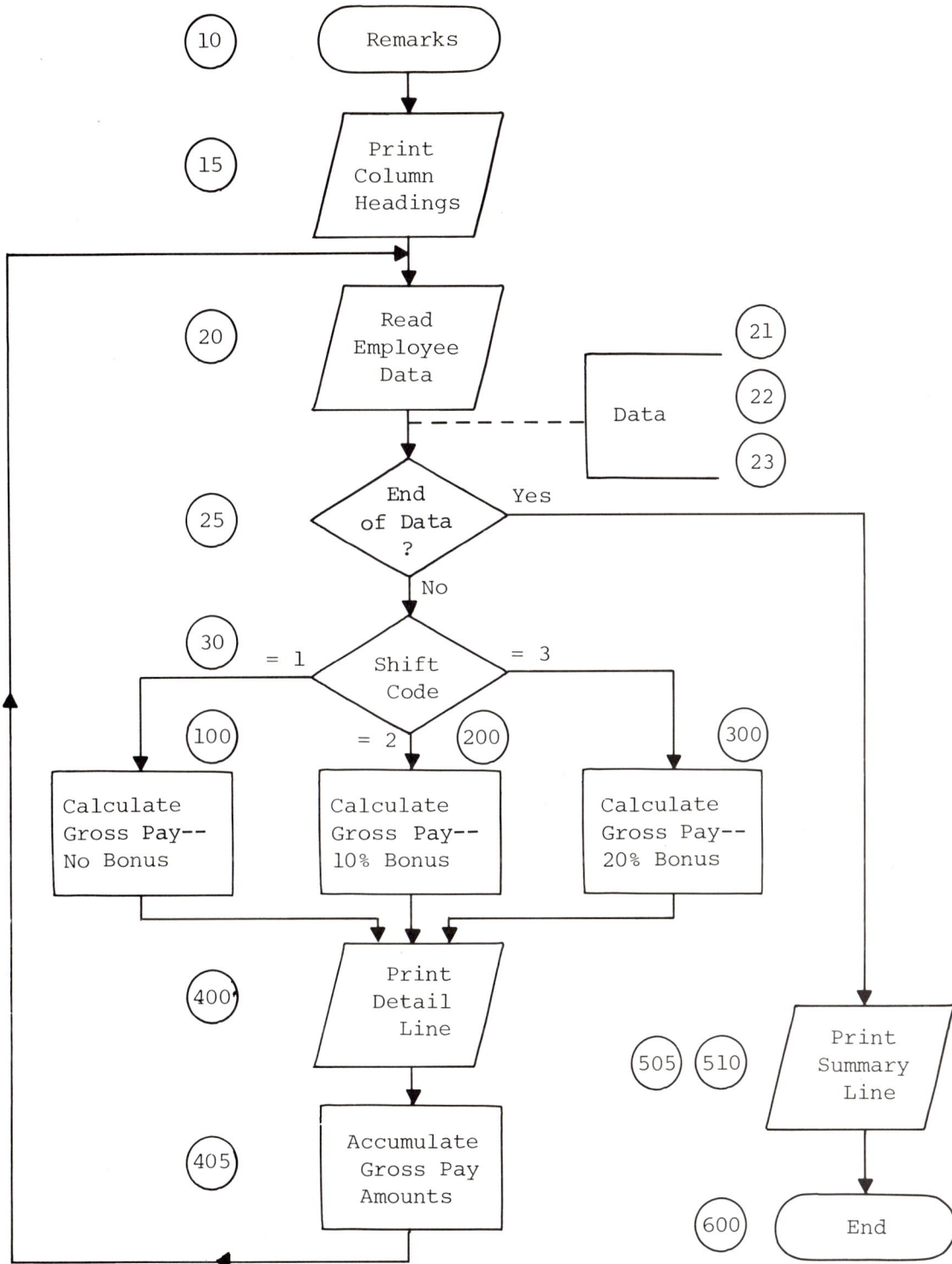

Figure 2-5

Program Flowchart—Payroll Report

data in lines 21, 22, and 23 may be stored in the cell.
Then at line 30 a new conditional transfer statement
is used.  (These new statements will be explained in
the next section.)

You should follow the rest of the programming steps that
we discussed in Chapter 1.  You might try to run the BASIC
program in Figure 2-6 to find out the characteristics of your
computer system.

```
10    REM CALCULATE EMPLOYEES GROSS PAY AND TOTAL PAY
15    PRINT "           EMPLOYEE NAME              GROSS PAY"
20    READ N$, S, H, R
21    DATA "JOHN JONES", 1, 40, 5.25, "BILL ADAMS", 3, 38.2, 4.50
22    DATA "MARY SMITH", 3, 36.5, 5.25, "JIM WILLIAMS", 2, 41.3, 3.40
23    DATA "ALICE DOWNS", 2, 37.1, 4.33, "ALL DONE", 0, 0, 0
25    IF S = 0 THEN 500
30    ON S GO TO 100, 200, 300
100   LET G = H * R
105   GO TO 400
200   LET G = H * R * 1.10
205   GO TO 400
300   LET G = H * R * 1.20
400   PRINT TAB (12): N$: TAB(34): "$"; G
405   LET T = T + G
410   GO TO 20
500   PRINT
505   PRINT USING 510, T
510   :           THE TOTAL PAY FOR ALL EMPLOYEES IS $#####.##
600   END
```

Figure 2-6

BASIC Program—Payroll Report

EXPLANATION OF BASIC STATEMENTS

Several new BASIC statements are introduced in this
program.  But you should know the meaning of the statements
at lines 10, 25, 100, 105, 200, 205, 300, 405, 410, and 600.
You should also be able to write similar statements that will
tell the computer to do similar things.  If you are not sure
of each of these statements, please return to Chapter 1 and
review.

> Remember, you are learning a "foreign" language,
> and you must know the first stage before you can
> go on to the second stage, just like climbing the
> rungs of a ladder.

Now that you are sure you know, we can go on to the second
stage.

## Printing Headings and Messages

```
   . . .
10 . . .
15 PRINT "          EMPLOYEE NAME          GROSS PAY"
20 . . .
```

Line 15 will cause the computer to print two column
headings.  Headings and messages are usually enclosed in
quotation marks and may be spaced across the page by leaving
blank spaces between the first quote mark and the start of
the column heading, as shown in line 15.

> Some systems allow only a single quote or
> apostrophe.

Also, by leaving blank spaces between the first and second
column headings, you can space the second heading farther
across the page.  Line 15 will cause the printer to indent
EMPLOYEE NAME ten spaces and to leave ten blank spaces between
the two headings as follows:

```
                                                      Print
1            15            30            45          Positions
_____
        EMPLOYEE NAME              GROSS PAY
```

You should notice that the quotation marks override the
automatic print zone spacing.  The heading EMPLOYEE NAME
uses the last five spaces of print zone 1 and the first
eight spaces of print zone 2.
    If you want your column headings to be printed on two

lines in the first and second print zones, you would write
the following BASIC statements:

```
15   PRINT "EMPLOYEE", "GROSS"
16   PRINT " NAME", " PAY"
```

The output would be

| 1 | 15 | 30 | 45 | Print Positions |
|---|----|----|----|-----------------|
| EMPLOYEE | GROSS | | | |
| NAME | PAY | | | |

Notice that we must code one PRINT statement for each line
we wish to print.  By placing blank spaces between the opening
quote and the heading, we are able to center the second line
of the heading under the longer first line headings.  Also
remember that commas cause the output to be printed in the
15-space print zones.

Here is another example.  If you want to print a message
and the total amount owed by the grocery customer in Chapter 1,
you should write the following PRINT statement:

```
50   PRINT "THE TOTAL AMOUNT OWED FOR YOUR GROCERIES IS $"; T
```

Your computer will print the message and the value stored in
T as follows:

| 1 | 15 | 30 | 45 | Print Positions |
|---|----|----|----|-----------------|
| THE TOTAL AMOUNT OWED FOR YOUR GROCERIES IS $9.41 | | | | |

Notice that the message starts at the first print position and
continues through the second and third print zones.  Also,
you should observe that the quotations marks are <u>not</u> printed.

If you look carefully at line 50, you will see a semicolon
following the ending quotation mark.  When you use a semicolon
this way, you tell the printer to leave only two or three
spaces between printed values.  In other words, this is
another way to override the normal 15-space print zone.  For

example, assume A = 25, B = 98.75, and C = 1.33.  If you write

    120  PRINT A, B, C

the output will look like this:

```
                                                    Print
1            15           30           45           Positions
_____
25           98.75        1.33
```

But if you write

    120  PRINT A; B; C

the output will look like this:

```
                                                    Print
1              15         30          45            Positions
_____
25  98.75  1.33
```

The general form of the PRINT statement when used for headings and messages is

| | | |
|---|---|---|
| 1- | Line number | Must precede all BASIC statements. |
| 2- | PRINT | Key word which activates the output device. |
| 3- | Heading or message | Specifies actual words and spaces to be printed.  Must be enclosed in quotation marks and may be separated with commas or semicolons.  Messages and variables may be included in the same PRINT statement. |

Now It's Your Turn

1- Assume you want to print a report title, PAYROLL REPORT, for the sample problem.  You want to center the title over the column headings.  Write the BASIC statement that will cause the computer to print this report title.

_____

*****

```
5  PRINT "                    PAYROLL REPORT"
```

By leaving 20 blank spaces between the beginning quote mark
and the report title, we can move the title over the center
of our output line.

2- You want to print an accounts receivable report.  This
report should include a report title and the following column
headings:  customer name, previous balance, purchases,
payments, and current balance.  You should center the title
and space the column headings across 60 or 70 spaces.

_____
_____
_____
_____
_____

*****

   You need to be careful with this one to be certain you
don't write any statement that goes beyond space 72.

```
 5  PRINT "                        ACCOUNTS RECEIVABLE REPORT"
15  PRINT "CUSTOMER" "PREVIOUS", " ", " ", "CURRENT"
16  PRINT "  NAME", "BALANCE", "PURCHASES", "PAYMENTS", "BALANCE"
```

This program segment will cause the computer to print the
following:

```
                    ACCOUNTS RECEIVABLE REPORT

CUSTOMER        PREVIOUS                              CURRENT
  NAME          BALANCE     PURCHASES     PAYMENTS    BALANCE
```

Notice the "empty" quote marks in line 15.  These cause the
computer to skip the third and fourth print zones and to
place the heading CURRENT in the fifth zone.

Back to the Sample Problem—Using Alphabetic DATA

```
15  . . .
20  READ N$, S, H, R
21  DATA "JOHN JONES", 1, 40, 5.25, . . .
22  . . .
```

   Most business problems require the use of alphabetic
data.  A payroll report, for instance, should include each

employee's name.  And an accounts receivable report would
not be complete without each customer's name.

In the READ statement at line 20, the variable N$ tells
the computer that alphabetic data are to be read and stored
in the storage area named N$.  The variable N$ is called a
string variable.  It consists of a letter of the alphabet
followed by a dollar sign.  The following are correct string
variables:  A$, C$, X$, Q$.

Here are some incorrect string variables along with the
reason each is incorrect:

| | |
|---|---|
| AB$ | More than one letter. |
| Z | No dollar sign; will only accept numeric values. |
| 2C$ | Begins with a digit. |
| $R | Begins with a dollar sign. |

When line 20 is first executed, the computer will select
the first four data elements from the DATA statement at
line 21, and CPU storage will be

| N$ | S | H | R |
|---|---|---|---|
| JOHN JONES | 1 | 40 | 5.25 |

The rules and relationships between READ and DATA
statements are the same as those discussed in Chapter 1.

When you wish to enter alphabetic data into a program,
you use a string variable in the READ statement.  And you
must be sure to enter the alphabetic data in the DATA
statement so that it will work on your computer.  If you
want to output that alphabetic data, you will use the same
string variable in a PRINT statement.  (More about this
later.)

A string variable may be used to store data that
contain both alphabetic and numeric values, such as a street
address.  The following program segment will cause the
computer to enter a name and address:

```
3  DATA "ALICE SMITH", "2538 HARBOR ROAD", "BOSTON  MASS"
5  READ X$, Y$, Z$
```

The string variable X$ will contain ALICE SMITH, Y$ will

contain 2538 HARBOR ROAD, and Z$ will contain BOSTON MASS.
Notice that there is no comma between the city and the state.
A comma there would indicate the start of a new data
element, and we don't want that here.

Not all computer systems use the same method for
programming alphabetic data.  Figure 2-7 shows some of the
variations used for handling alphabetic data.  You should
check on this in the BASIC programming manual for the
computer you are using.

| Manufacturer | Maximum Number of Characters | Specifying Length of String | Alphabetic Data in DATA Statement |
|---|---|---|---|
| CDC | 78 | none | JOHN JONES |
| Honeywell 400 Series | 132 | none | JOHN JONES |
| Hewlett Packard 2000 | 72 | DIM N$ (20) | "JOHN JONES" |
| Digital Equipment | | | |
|   PDP-11 | 255 | none | "JOHN JONES" |
| Data General | No restriction | DIM N$ (20) | "JOHN JONES" |
| General Automation | 72 | DIM N$ (20) | "JOHN JONES" |
| Xerox Sigma 5 & 9 | 132 | none | "JOHN JONES" |
| Varian 73 | No string capability available | | |
| IBM 370 VSBASIC | 18 | none | 'JOHN JONES' |
| IBM 5100 | 18 | none | 'JOHN JONES' |

Figure 2-7

Methods for Programming Alphabetic Data

Now It's Your Turn

1- Assume you want to print name and address labels for
mailing.  You therefore want to enter the name of each person,
the street address, and the name of the city and state with
the zip code.  Write the BASIC statements that will cause
the computer to enter the data for each person.  Line 5 is a
sample DATA statement.

    5  DATA "JOHN JONES", "2351 ELM STREET", "GOLDEN COLORADO 80401"


   20  _____

*****

   20  READ N$, C$, S$

2-  Now you want to cause the computer to print the address
label which should consist of three lines, as follows:

    JOHN JONES
    2351 ELM STREET
    GOLDEN COLORADO   80401

Write the BASIC statement(s) that will cause the computer to
print out the address label.

_____

_____

_____

*****

    100   PRINT N$
    101   PRINT C$
    102   PRINT S$

## Back to the Sample Program

Lines 21, 22, and 23 of the sample program include the
test data for five employees.  The ALL DONE data set is the
"dummy" data we will use to signal the end of the data in the
IF statement at line 25.  If you are not sure about line 25,
please review the discussion of the IF statement in Chapter 1.

## The ON. . .GO TO Statement

```
   .
  25  . . .
  30  ON S GO TO 100, 200, 300
 100  . . .
   .
```

The ON. . .GO TO statement at line 30 is another kind of
conditional transfer and is often called the computed GO TO.
The variable S contains a value representing the shift
worked by an employee.  This value may be 1, 2, or 3.  The
three numbers following GO TO are line numbers to which the
program will branch.  The particular line number depends on
the value stored in S when the statement is executed.  For
example, if S = 1, the computer will branch to the <u>first</u>

line number in the list, line 100 in this example.  If
S = 3, the computer will branch to the <u>third</u> line number,
line 300.  In this sample program, there are only three
shifts; therefore we need to program a three-way branch.  The
ON...GO TO statement does this for us.

   This branch could have been coded using IF-THEN statements as follows:

```
     .
    30  IF S = 1 THEN 100
    31  IF S = 2 THEN 200
    32  IF S = 3 THEN 300
   100  LET G = etc.
     .
     .
```

But if we wish to branch eight ways, the IF-THEN method
becomes very inefficient.

   An additional example may help you to understand the
advantage of the ON...GO TO statement.  Assume we wish to
analyze sales for eight territories which are numbered
between 101 and 899 as follows:

   The hundreds position indicates the territory.
   The tens and units positions indicate the saleman number.

For example, 345 would indicate territory 3 and salesman 45.
We will input the code number using the variable N.  The
ON...GO TO statement that will cause this eight-way branch is

```
   25  ON N/100 GO TO 50, 65, 70, 90, 100, 102, 209, 219
```

   In this example, the computer will divide N by 100, keep
the whole number part of the answer, and cause a branch to
the appropriate line number.  If, for instance, N = 345, the
computer will divide 345 by 100, getting an answer of 3.45.
Only the 3 will be saved, and the computer will branch to the
third line number in the list, line 70 in the above example.

   You should note that you may use either a variable or an

arithmetic expression following the ON.  The value of the
variable or expression <u>may not be less than 1 or more than
the number of line numbers</u> following the GO TO.  If S in
line 30 of the sample program were to equal 5, the computer
would print the following error message:  ON EXPRESSION OUT
OF RANGE.  .(CDC).

> On some computer systems, the program will
> continue to the statement following the ON...GO TO
> statement when the value of the variable or
> expression is greater than the number of line
> numbers listed after GO TO.

The major advantage of the ON...GO TO statement is that a
multiple-way branch can be programmed with only one statement.
The disadvantage is that the variable or expression following
ON must be within the range of 1 to the number of line numbers
provided in the statement.  You should be careful to be sure
that the variable or expression following ON will equal 1, 2,
3, ... or <u>n</u>, where <u>n</u> is the number of line numbers given in
the statement.

The general form of the ON...GO TO statement is

| | | |
|---|---|---|
| 1- | Line number | Must precede all BASIC statements. |
| 2- | ON | Key word indicating conditional branch. |
| 3- | Variable or arithmetic expression | Specifies which of the list of line numbers following GO TO will be used.  Must have a value from 1 to number of line numbers listed. |
| 4- | GO TO | Indicates a branch to one of the line numbers listed. |
| 5- | Two or more line numbers | Specify points in program to which program is to branch. |

The varian 73 and the Hewlett Packard 2000
computer systems use a different command to
accomplish the multiple branch.  Line 30 of the
sample program would be coded as follows:

>     30  GO TO S OF 100, 200, 300

If S = 2, the computer will branch to the second
line number in series following OF, line 200,
in this example.

The IBM 5100 uses still a different statement
to program the multiple transfer.  Line 30 of
the sample program would be written as

>     30  GO TO 100, 200, 300, ON S

When S = 3, the computer will transfer to the
third line number, 300.

## Now It's Your Turn

1-  Write the BASIC statement that will cause the computer
to branch to other statements which will accumulate sales
amounts for each of 12 territories.  The input will consist
of one data set for each sale, including a territory code
numbered from 1 to 12 and a dollar amount of the sale.

---

*****

>     30  ON T GO TO 40, 45, 50, 55, 60, 65, 70, 75, 80, 85, 90, 95

Make sure you have 12 different line numbers following the
GO TO.

2-  You want to analyze customer credit performance based on
customer age.  The age groups are 20-29, 30-39, 40-49,
50-59, and 60-69.  Write a BASIC statement to cause the
computer to branch so that the needed calculations can be
made for each age group.  Watch out for this one!

---

*****

One way you could have written this is

    10   ON A / 10 - 1 GO TO 20, 30, 40, 50, 60

Assume that A = 26.  We want to branch to line 20 to make
the 20-29 calculation.  If we divide 26 by 10, the answer
is 2.6.  By subtracting the 1, our answer becomes 1.6; the
computer saves the 1 and branches to the first line number.

> The value of the line numbers in the ON...GO TO
> statement makes no difference in the program.
> In line 10 above, the line numbers could have
> been 11, 12, 13, and 15.  It is the left-to-
> right position of the numbers that is
> important.

Back to the Sample Program

```
 30   .
100   LET G = H * R
105   GO TO 400
200   LET G = H * R * 1.10
205   GO TO 400
300   LET G = H * R * 1.20
400   . . .
```

Remember, the program transferred to line 100 when S = 1:
the day shift.  These employees receive no bonus; therefore,
the gross pay calculation is hours worked times the pay rate.
Notice the GO TO 400 at line 105.  After we have computed the
gross pay for day shift employees, we must be sure to skip to
the PRINT statement at line 400.

Line 200 calculates the gross pay and 10% bonus for swing
shift employees, and line 300 calculates the gross pay plus
20% for graveyard shift people.

Spacing Printed Output—the TAB Function

```
      .
300   . . .
400   PRINT TAB(12); N$, TAB(34); "$"; G
405   . . .
      .
```

Line 400 will cause the computer to print one detail line

for each employee.  Remember that each detail line is to
consist of the employee's name and the gross pay.  In this
example, N$ is the storage area in which the employee's name
is stored.  The TAB(12); N$ will cause the computer to skip
or tabulate to the twelfth print position and to print the
employee's name.  The TAB(34); "$"; G will cause a dollar
sign to be printed in the thirty-fourth position followed
by the gross pay amount stored in G.

The detail lines will look like this:

```
                                                    Print
1          10        20        30        40         Positions
_____

           JOHN JONES            $ 210
           BILL ADAMS            $ 206.28
           MARY SMITH            $ 229.95
           JIM WILLIAMS          $ 154.462
           ALICE DOWNS           $ 176.707
```

As you can see, the TAB function overrides the
automatic zone spacing and causes the printer to tabulate or
skip to the print position specified by the number in the
parentheses.  You may write your program so that a number is
used, as in this example.  Or you may use a variable in the
parentheses.  Here is an example using a variable:

```
1000  PRINT TAB(N); X
```

If N = 17 and X = 2.314, the printer will print 2.314
starting in position 17.  Or you may use an arithmetic
expression in the parentheses, like this:

```
1200  PRINT TAB(N - 5); X
```

Assuming the same values for N and X, the printer will print
2.314 at position 12, (17 - 5).

You may also use the TAB function to space headings.  For
example, the column headings required for the sample program
could be printed using the following PRINT statement:

```
15  PRINT TAB(10); "EMPLOYEE NAME"; TAB(33); "GROSS PAY"
```

The printed output will be the same as that shown on page 65.

The general form of the TAB function is

| | | |
|---|---|---|
| 1- | Line number | Must precede all BASIC statements. |
| 2- | PRINT | Key word specifying output. |
| 3- | TAB (expression) | Key word which establishes the print position to be used, based on the value of the expression enclosed in parentheses. |
| 4- | Simple or string variable, headings, message | Usually separated by semi-colons; specifies what is to be printed. |

Now It's Your Turn

1- Write the BASIC statement(s) that will cause the computer to print the report title and column headings for Figure 2-1. Space your output over at least 60 print positions using the TAB function.

_____

_____

_____

*****

```
10   PRINT TAB(20); "PAYROLL REGISTER"
15   PRINT TAB(3); "NAME"; TAB(16); "GROSS PAY"; TAB(33); "INCOME TAX";
16   PRINT TAB(48); "NET PAY"
```

This is one way you could tell the computer to print the title and four column headings. The "trailing" or "dangling" semicolon at the end of line 15 keeps the printer from spacing to the next print line and tells the printer to print NET PAY on the same line as the other column headings starting at position 48.

Of course, this approach isn't fair to you because we haven't discussed that aspect of the PRINT statement. So here is how you should have written this program segment:

```
10   PRINT TAB(20); "PAYROLL REGISTER"
15   PRINT TAB(16); "GROSS"; TAB(33); "INCOME"; TAB(48); "NET"
16   PRINT TAB(3); "NAME"; TAB(17); "PAY"; TAB(35); "TAX"; TAB(48); "PAY"
```

This will print two-line column headings as follows:

| 1 | 10 | 20 | 30 | 40 | 50 | 60 | Print Positions |
|---|----|----|----|----|----|----|-----------------|
|   |    | GROSS |  | INCOME |  | NET |  |
| NAME | | PAY | | TAX | | PAY | |

## Back to the Sample Program

Line 405 is our "adding machine" to accumulate the total of all gross pay amounts.  This is almost the same statement that we used in the grocery check-out problem in Chapter 1. Remember?

Line 410 closes the program loop by returning the program back to line 20.  Please notice that this loop includes the input, process, and output of each employee's payroll data. The loop does not include the column headings or the summary line.

## Controlling Vertical Spacing

```
410  . . .
500  PRINT
505  . . .
```

You have learned to control horizontal spacing across the output line by using commas and semicolons as separators and by using the TAB function.  Line 500 shows one way to control vertical spacing.  The "empty" PRINT statement tells the computer to print a blank line which will leave a space between the last detail line and the summary lines, as follows:

```
ALICE DOWNS           $ 276.707

THE TOTAL PAY FOR ALL EMPLOYEES IS $  977.40
```

If you want to leave two blank lines between the column headings and the first detail line in the sample program, you should add these statements:

```
15  PRINT "        EMPLOYEE NAME       GROSS PAY"
16  PRINT
17  PRINT
20  . . .
```

Each "empty" PRINT statement will cause the printer to output a blank line.

However, in some cases, we will want to stop the printer from spacing so that we can print several values on one line.  You were given a preview of this when I used the "dangling" semicolon in my answer to the exercise on page 77. You may also use a "dangling" comma as in the following program:

```
 5   READ A, B, C
 6   DATA 2.5, 3.95, 1.8
10   PRINT A,
20   PRINT B,
30   PRINT C
40   END
```

The output line for this program will look like this:

|   |    |    | Print |
|---|----|----|-------|
| 1 | 15 | 30 | Positions |
| 2.5 | 3.95 | 1.8 | |

If lines 10 and 20 were written without the dangling commas, the output would have been placed on three lines in the first print zone as follows:

|   |    |    | Print |
|---|----|----|-------|
| 1 | 15 | 30 | Positions |
| 2.5 | | | |
| 3.95 | | | |
| 1.8 | | | |

Remember, you can control horizontal spacing by using commas, semicolons, and the TAB function.  You can control vertical spacing by using "empty" PRINT statements or by using dangling commas or semicolons.

Editing Printed Output—the PRINT USING Statement

```
     .
405   . . .
505   PRINT USING 510, T
510   :        THE TOTAL PAY FOR ALL EMPLOYEES IS $#####.##
600   . . .
```

The PRINT USING gives us still another way to control an

output line. Lines 505 and 510 work together as a pair. Line
505 tells the computer to use the <u>line image</u> shown in line 510
and to print the value stored in T in the space provided by
the #####.## in line 510. In other words, line 510 gives an
image or picture of what the print line should look like,
including the message and spaces for numeric values: Lines
505 and 510 tell the computer to print the following:

| | | | | | | Print Positions |
|---|---|---|---|---|---|---|
| 1 | 10 | 20 | 30 | 40 | 50 | |

THE TOTAL PAY FOR ALL EMPLOYEES IS $  977.40

In this example, the image indicates that the message
should be indented six spaces. Notice that there are six
spaces between the colon and the start of the message but
that the message is <u>not</u> enclosed in quotation marks. And
each # (pound sign) provides space for one character,
either numeric or alphabetic. In line 510, five dollar
values and two cent values may be printed. By limiting the
cent positions, we tell the computer to round the total
from 977.399 to 977.40. The colon following the line number
is required as a separator between the line number and the
line image.

You may also use the PRINT USING statement to print
detail lines and headings. For example, the detail lines
required for the sample program could be printed with the
following statements:

```
400  PRINT USING 401, N$, G
401  :              ##############        $####.##
```

The detail line output will be slightly different from that
shown on page 76 because there are only two cent positions.
The output will be

```
                    JOHN JONES      $ 210.00
                    BILL ADAMS      $ 206.28
                    MARY SMITH      $ 229.95
                    JIM WILLIAMS    $ 154.46
                    ALICE DOWNS     $ 176.71
```

The variables N$ and G in line 400 are the same as those

in the sample program.  Line 401 gives the desired spacing just
as the TAB(12) and TAB(34) in the sample program.  Fifteen spaces
are allowed for the string variable, the 15 #'s.  The dollar
sign is included as part of the image.  Four dollar digits and
two cent digits are provided by ####.##.  Notice that the gross
pay for Alice Downs is rounded and that the zero cents are
included in John Jones pay.

> The PRINT USING statements shown above are
> available for Control Data, IBM 370 and 5100,
> Honeywell 400, and Xerox Sigma 5 and 9
> computer systems.
>
> A different form of the PRINT USING is
> available for the PDP-11, the Hewlett Packard
> 2000, and the Data General systems.  Many
> computer systems do not support this feature
> of the BASIC language.  You should check the
> BASIC programming manual for the computer
> system you are using.

The general form of the PRINT USING statement is

| | | |
|---|---|---|
| 1- | Line number | Must precede all BASIC statements. |
| 2- | PRINT USING | Key words indicating the use of an image or picture line. |
| 3- | Line number | Line number of the image line. |
| 4- | Variables | Specifies what the computer is to print.  Values will be inserted in the image line in the same order that the variables occur in the PRINT USING line. |

The general form of the image line is

| | | |
|---|---|---|
| 1- | Line number | Must precede all BASIC statements; must be same number as that following PRINT USING. |
| 2- | : | Colon must separate line number from image. |
| 3- | Image of print line | Message, headings, at least one # (pound sign) for each digit or character; one set of #'s for each variable listed in the PRINT USING statement. |

Now It's Your Turn

1-  Write the BASIC statements that will tell the computer
to print the report title and column headings for Figure 2-1.
Space your output over at least 60 print positions.  Use the
PRINT USING statements.

_____

_____

_____

_____

*****

There are two ways you could solve this problem.

```
500   PRINT USING 501
501   :                    PAYROLL REGISTER
505   PRINT USING 506
506   :   NAME         GROSS PAY         INCOME TAX      NET PAY
```

Or you could have written 505 and 506 like this:

```
505   PRINT USING 506
506   :             GROSS                 INCOME          NET
507   PRINT USING 508
508   :   NAME      PAY                   TAX             PAY
```

You should notice that when we print headings, we do not include
any variables in the PRINT USING statements.


NOW IT'S YOUR TURN PROBLEM—EXPANDED PAYROLL

The problem you are going to program now is a modification
of the sample problem in this chapter.  To make this problem
a little more realistic, we will add the income tax
calculations and deductions.  The employees' gross pay will be
calculated just as in the sample program in lines 30 through
300.  We will insert the tax calculations before we print the
detail lines.

We will make an assumption that an employee's gross pay

will never be less than $100 or more that $499 per week.  The
tax rates are as follows:

| Gross Pay | Tax Rate |
|---|---|
| $100-$199 | 10% of gross pay |
| $200-$299 | 12% of gross pay |
| $300-$399 | 15% of gross pay |
| $400-$499 | 20% of gross pay |

This report should include the following column headings:
EMPLOYEE NAME, GROSS PAY, INCOME TAX DEDUCTION, and NET PAY.
The income tax deduction will be calculated by multiplying
the tax rate by the gross pay.  The net pay will be the gross
pay minus the income tax deduction.  We will also want to
accumulate totals for gross pay, income tax, and net pay.
The summary line will include the message TOTALS and the
three values.

Figure 2-8 is a program flowchart that gives us a
planned solution to this problem.

Remember, you are supposed to honestly try to
write each line before you look at the suggested
coding of the BASIC statement.  If you are not
sure, please refer to the appropriate section in
this chapter or in Chapter 1.

Line 15:  The first thing you need to do is to tell the
computer to print the column headings.  You may use any of
the three techniques you learned in Chapter 2.  Because of
the number of characters, I suggest you print two lines.

_____

_____

_____

_____

*****

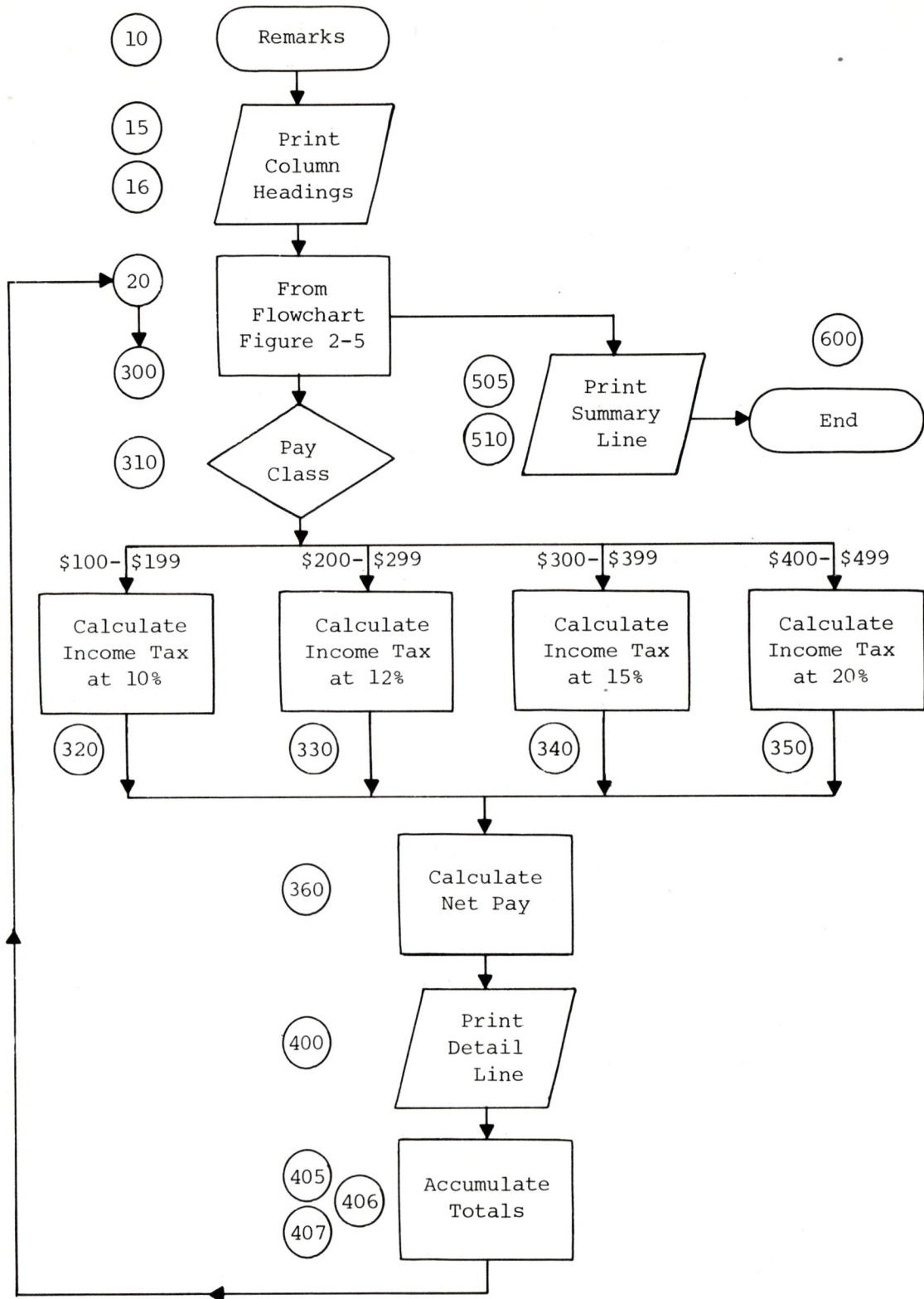

Figure 2-8

Program Flowchart—Expanded Payroll

```
15   PRINT "EMPLOYEE", "GROSS", "INCOME TAX", "NET"
16   PRINT "  NAME", " PAY", "DEDUCTION", "PAY"
```

This is the simplest way to print these headings.  However, you could have tried the PRINT USING statements, like this:

```
15   PRINT USING 16
16   :   EMPLOYEE        GROSS      INCOME TAX      NET
17   PRINT USING 18
18   :    NAME            PAY       DEDUCTIONS      PAY
```

But you should have found out that the PRINT TAB will not work.  There will be more than 72 characters in each BASIC statement.

Lines 20-300:  These statements can be used as is except for lines 105 and 205.  If you look at Figure 2-8, you will notice that these lines should be  GO TO 310.

Line 310:  Your job now is to write a BASIC statement that will tell the computer to decide which pay classification to assign to an employee.  If you are not sure how to do this one, I suggest you review pages 71 through 73.

```
310 _____
```
*****

Here is what you should have written:

```
310  ON G / 100 GO TO 320, 330, 340, 350
```

Remember, we calculated the employee's gross pay, G, at line 300.  If the computer divides that value by 100, it will save either a 1, 2, 3, or 4.  If the "saved" value equals 1, we want to branch to line 320 to calculate the income tax deduction at 10%.  The ON...GO TO statement will do just that.

Line 320:  You want to tell the computer to calculate the income tax deduction and store the answer in D for deduction, using the 10% tax rate.

```
320 _____
```
*****

This should have been easy for you:

```
320  LET D = G * .10
```

Remember, you must convert the 10% into a decimal value.

<u>Line 325</u>:  This line isn't specified on the flowchart, but
it is absolutely essential to correct answers.

    325 _____

*****

    The arrow flowing from the "calculate income tax" process
symbol should have helped you with this statement:

    325  GO TO 360

<u>Lines 330, 335, 340, 345, 350</u>:  You should have no trouble
with these.

    330 _____
    335 _____
    340 _____
    345 _____
    350 _____

*****

    Lines 320 and 325 should have been used as examples.

    330  LET D = G * .12
    335  GO TO 360
    340  LET D = G * .15
    345  GO TO 360
    350  LET D = G * .20

Please notice that you must include the GO TO 360 after the
tax deduction calculations.  But why not a GO TO 360 at
line 355?

<u>Line 360</u>:  This should be simple for you.

    360 _____
*****

    360  LET N = G - D

It is all right to use the variable N for <u>n</u>et pay.  The computer
knows that N and N$ are different variables and therefore unique.

<u>Line 400</u>:  You want to tell the computer to print the detail
line which includes the employee's name, his gross pay, his
income tax deduction, and his net pay.  Remember that we input
the employee's name at line 20 and that we calculated the
other values.

400 _____

_____

*****

I think you should have used PRINT USING statements like
this:

```
400  PRINT USING 401 N$, G, D, N
401  :##############      $###.##      $###.##         $###.##
```

But it depends on how you wrote the column headings.  If you
used the first method I illustrated at lines 15 and 16, then
your PRINT statement should be

```
400  PRINT N$, G, D, N
```

However, this will not center the values under the column
headings, nor will it print the dollar signs or the two
decimal values.

<u>Lines 405, 406, 407</u>:  The program flowchart indicates that
you are to accumulate totals for gross pay, income tax
deductions, and net pay.  All you have to do is set up three
"adding machines" for your accumulations.

405 _____

406 _____

407 _____

*****

```
405  LET T1 = T1 + G
406  LET T2 = T2 + D
407  LET T3 = T3 + N
```

You could have used different variables as your "adding machines," but you must be sure you have not used the same variable somewhere else in this program.

Line 410:  This line is the same used in the sample program:

    410   GO TO 20

Lines 505, 510:  These lines should output the summary line, the word TOTALS, and the three accumulated totals.  I suggest you use PRINT USING so that your total values are lined up with your detail line columns.

    505 _____
    510 _____
*****

Your statements should look like this:

    505   PRINT USING 510 T1, T2, T3
    510   :      TOTALS        $####.##      $###.##      $####.##

You should pay particular attention to the horizontal spacing in line 510.  The accumulated values should be printed so that their decimal points are in the same position as those in the detail lines.  Of course, if you used the "regular" PRINT statement, you can assure that your values are aligned.

After you have finished your expanded program, it should look like the one in Figure 2-9.  This program will include the appropriate statements from Figure 2-6.


SUMMARY

In this chapter, we have been working on the printing of business reports.  These reports usually include headings, subheadings, several detail lines, and often a summary line.

Two programming concepts were discussed.  Headings, subheadings, and summary lines should be printed only once

```
10    REM CALCULATE EMPLOYEES GROSS PAY, INCOME TAX, AND NET PAY
15    PRINT USING 16
16    :    EMPLOYEE           GROSS       INCOME TAX          NET
17    PRINT USING 18
18    :       NAME            PAY         DEDUCTIONS          PAY
20    READ N$, S, H, R
21    DATA "JOHN JONES", 1, 40, 5.25, "BILL ADAMS", 3, 38.2, 4.50
22    DATA "MARY SMITH", 3, 36.5, 5.25, "JIM WILLIAMS", 2, 41.3, 3.40
23    DATA "ALICE DOWNS", 2, 37.1, 4.33, "ALL DONE", 0, 0, 0
25    IF S = 0 THEN 500
30    ON S GO TO 100, 200, 300
100   LET G = H * R
105   GO TO 310
200   LET G = H * R * 1.10
205   GO TO 310
300   LET G = H * R * 1.20
310   ON G/100 GO TO 320, 330, 340, 350
320   LET D = G * .10
325   GO TO 360
330   LET D = G * .12
335   GO TO 360
340   LET D = G * .15
345   GO TO 360
350   LET D = G * .20
360   LET N = G - D
400   PRINT USING  401 N$, G, D, N
401   :##############    $###.##      $###.##         $###.##
405   LET T1 = T1 + G
406   LET T2 = T2 + D
407   LET T3 = T3 + N
410   GO TO 20
500   PRINT
505   PRINT USING 510 T1, T2, T3
510   :    TOTALS        $####.##      $###.##        $####.##
520   END
```

Figure 2-9

Now It's Your Turn Problem—Expanded Payroll

and therefore should be coded <u>outside</u> the loop that produces
the detail lines.  The second concept was program sequence or
logic.  Sometimes a program will "run" but will print out
incorrect answers.  You should make sure that the program
sequence will produce the answers you want by using GO TO
statements.

The new BASIC statements that have been presented in this chapter are summarized below:

1- PRINT            Output statement; prints headings, detail lines, and summary lines.  May be used to alter spacing or edit output.

   line number    PRINT    heading or message enclosed in quotes

   line number    PRINT TAB (expression); heading, message, variable(s)

   line number    PRINT USING   line number, variable(s)

   line number    :  line image    (used with PRINT USING statement)

2- READ             Input statement; names variables identifying CPU storage areas for both numeric and alphabetic data.

   line number    READ   numeric or string variable(s)

3- ON...GO TO       Conditional branch statement; causes computer to branch to any one of several line numbers following the GO TO depending on value of variable or expression following ON.

   line number    ON  variable, expression   GO TO several line numbers

EXERCISES

A-  Write the BASIC statements that will cause the computer to output a report title INVENTORY STATUS followed by four column headings:  ID NUMBER, ITEM DESCRIPTION, QUANTITY ON HAND, and QUANTITY ON ORDER.

   1-  Use PRINT statement(s) with automatic spacing.

2- Use PRINT TAB statement(s).

3- Use PRINT USING statements.

Space your output over at least 70 spaces, and leave one blank line between the title and column headings.  Also, leave a blank line before the detail lines.

B- We want to calculate sales discounts for our customers based on the amount of the sale, as follows:

| Amount of Sale | Discount Percent |
|----------------|------------------|
| $  0-$ 99      | 0%               |
| 100- 199       | 1                |
| 200- 299       | 3                |
| 300- 399       | 5                |

Write the BASIC statements that will cause the computer to branch to the different lines to make the discount calculation. We READ the amount of the sale into S.

1- Use the ON...GO TO statement(s).

2- Use IF-THEN statement(s).

C- Correct any errors in the following BASIC statements. Do not make any unnecessary corrections.

1-  15   READ A5, 6$, $AB

2-  30   GO TO 20, 45, 10, 17, ON X

3-  6  ON A2 THEN 10, 5, 1000, 10

4-  200  PRINT USING 200 $B, H, R, S$
    120 ;  ###    ##              ###              $##.##

5-  300  PRINT  "THE ANSWER IS";   TAB(5); X

6-  330  PRINT TAB(X);  "*"

PROBLEMS

1- Code a BASIC program that will prepare a weekly payroll
register.

Output      Report headings:
        PAYROLL REGISTER
          current date

         Column headings:

        EMPLOYEE NAME     HOURS WORKED     PAY RATE     GROSS PAY

         One detail line for each employee.

         Summary line:

        TOTAL GROSS PAY $-----.--     (align with GROSS PAY
                                     column)

Input       Current date (i.e., March 23, 1977).
         One record for each employee:
          Employee name
          Wage class (from 1 to 5)
          Hours worked

         Pay rate depends on the number of years worked:

| Years Worked | Pay Rate | Wage Class |
|---|---|---|
| 0-1 | $3.50 | 1 |
| 2-3 | $4.25 | 2 |
| 4-5 | $4.75 | 3 |
| 6-7 | $5.00 | 4 |
| 8 or more | $5.50 | 5 |

Process    Calculate gross pay (no overtime is paid).
         Accumulate gross pay amounts.

Transfer    Last employee?
         Wage class?

Test data    Current date

| Name | Wage Class | Hours |
|---|---|---|
| Alice Adams | 2 | 42.3 |
| John Jones | 4 | 39.5 |
| Walt Warren | 1 | 41.5 |
| Harry Hansen | 3 | 37.3 |
| Bill Brown | 2 | 48.3 |
| Mary Morris | 5 | 40.0 |
| Helen Harris | 4 | 36.9 |
| No More | 6 | 0 |

2-  Code a BASIC program that will prepare a monthly
customer billing report for NucElectric Co.  The company
charges its customers as follows:

    First  50 kWh used: 6.5 cents per kWh.
    Next 100 kWh: 5 cents per kWh.
    Next 200 kWh: 4.5 cents kWh.
    Over 350 kWh: 3 cents per kWh.

These charges are progressive.  For example, if a customer
used 180 kWh, the bill would be calculated as follows:

        First    50 kWh * .065 = $3.25
        Next    100 kWh * .05  =  5.00
        Next     30 kWh * .045 =  1.35
    Totals    180 kWh                $9.60

Output          Heading:  NUCELECTRIC CO.
                Subhead 1:  CUSTOMER BILLING      current month
                Subhead 2:  Column headings:
                        CUSTOMER NAME, ELECTRICITY USED, CHARGE
                One detail line for each customer:
                  Name
                  Kilowatt-hours used
                  Amount owed     ($---.--)
                Summary line:  TOTAL AMOUNT OWED      $---.-- (align
                  with charge)

Input           Current month.
                One record for each customer:
                  Customer name
                  Kilowatt-hours used

Process         Calculate bill for each customer.
                Accumulate total charged to all customers.

Transfer        Last customer?
                kWh used?

Test data       George Baker, 400
                Allen Hunt, 160
                Mary Wilson, 35
                Bob Cary, 85
                Henry Wilkes, 120
                Viola Bowers, 280
                No More, 0

3-  Code a BASIC program to prepare a delinquent accounts
receivable report.

Output          Heading:

                  DELINQUENT ACCOUNTS RECEIVABLE REPORT-current month
                Subheadings:

                                DAYS PAST DUE
                  NAME          30        60        90        120
                Detail line for each customer:
                  Name
                  Amount owed, under appropriate column headings, i.e.,
                    30-59 days past due under 30 days column.

                Summary line:

                  TOTALS      (accumulated amounts for each past due
                                period, aligned under detail columns)

Input           Current month.
                One record for each customer:
                  Name
                  Days past due
                  Amount owed

Process         Accumulate amounts in each past due category.

Transfer        Last customer?
                Days past due category?

Test data       Alice Adams         60        1025.50
                John Jones          30         250.75
                Walt Warren         67         195.50
                Harry Hansen       110          48.25
                Bill Brown          41          75.50
                Mary Morris        128         108.33
                Helen Harris        95         428.27
                No More            150           0

# 3

# FOR/NEXT Statements

So far, you have learned to write BASIC programs that will
solve typical business problems and to print business reports
with report titles, column headings, edited detail lines,
and summary lines.

   After you have completed this chapter, you will

1- Know how to use the FOR and NEXT statements to
   program predefined loops.  This is one of the most
   useful tools in programming.
2- Know another way of entering data using the INPUT
   statement.
3- Know another version of the PRINT statement.

Before getting into these new statements, however, we should
spend some time learning about program loops.


PROGRAMMING CONCEPTS

   In the sample programs in Chapters 1 and 2, we caused
the computer to loop using a GO TO statement to branch back
to a READ statement.  We ended the loop by using an IF-THEN
statement to test for the last data.  In this way, we were
able to input and process many records with only one READ
statement and several LET statements.  However, if a loop
were not possible, we would have had to repeat the READ and
LET statements for each grocery item or for each employee.

95

This would have been a very inefficient and dull way to solve
the problems.  Program loops are much more efficient.

There are two types of loops that may be used to solve
most business problems.  The most common, used for many
financial applications, is the input, process, output loop.
A second type, used for many statistical applications, is
the input, process loop.

Input, Process, Output Loop

A very common example of an input, process, output loop
is a payroll program.  The input consists of data about one
employee.  The process includes the calculation of his gross
pay, his income tax, etc.  The output is his paycheck.  The
program then branches back to carry out the entire payroll
operation for the next employee, until all employees' payroll
data have been processed.  Figure 3-1 shows this type of
program.

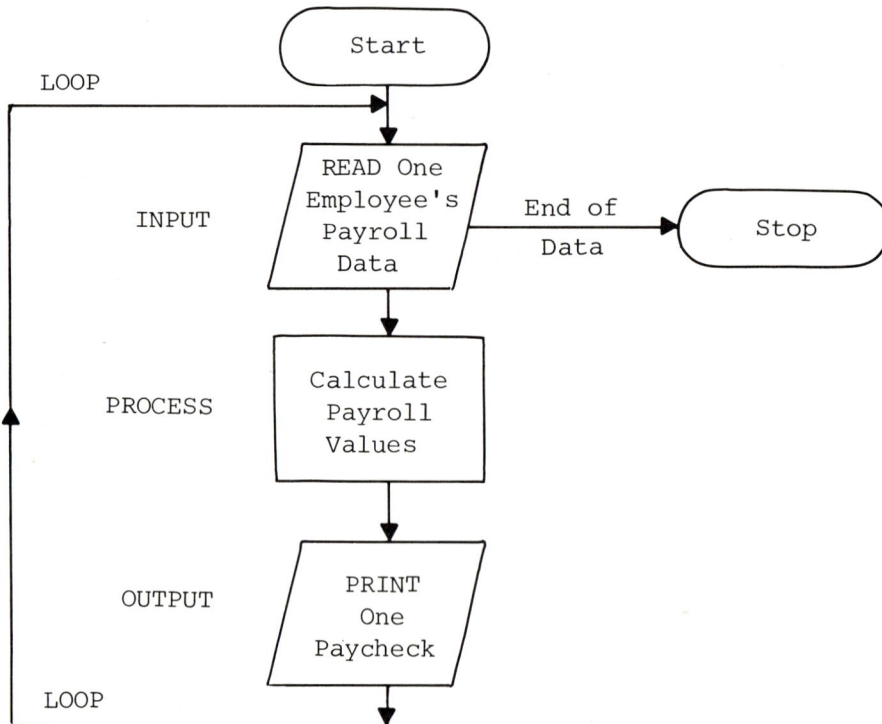

Figure 3-1
Input, Process, Output Loop

> Remember, be sure to put your headings and
> summary lines before and after the loop.

## Input, Process Loop

In this type of loop, all the input is processed. When
the loop is done, more processing usually occurs; then the
output is printed. The grocery check-out example in Chapter 1
is an example of this type of loop. In that program, the
loop consists of an input and a process and then a return to
the READ. The loop continues until all data are processed.
The program then branches to the PRINT statement to provide
the output. Figure 3-2 illustrates this type of loop.

> Notice that no detail lines are printed in this
> loop; only a summary line is printed after the
> "end of data" branch.

## Endless Loops

Many beginning programmers code a program so that the
computer performs an endless loop. An endless loop is one
that never stops; it just keeps going around and around. You

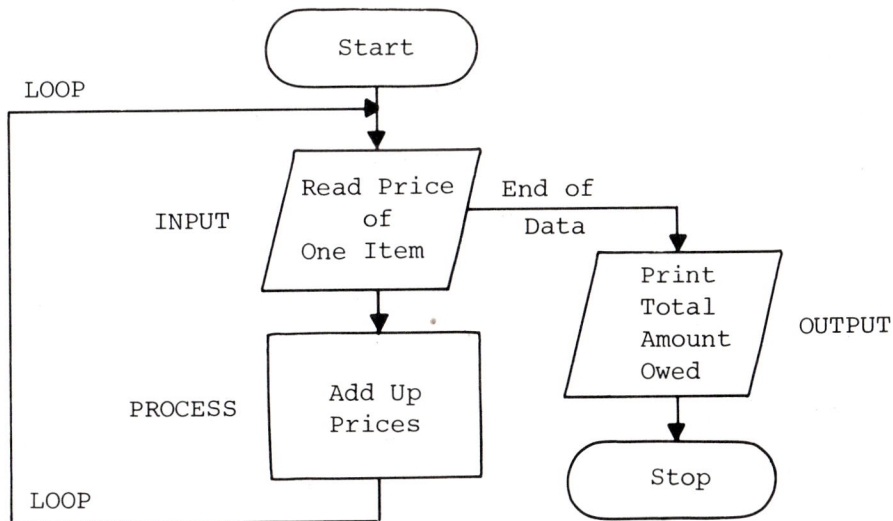

Figure 3-2

Input, Process Loop

must be sure that any loops in your programs will stop in some way.  The use of an IF-THEN statement to test for last data is one typical way to stop a loop.  But one of the best ways is to use the FOR and NEXT statements.  We will get to these in the next section.

> Please notice that the program flowcharts in Figures 3-1 and 3-2 both include an "end of data" branch to stop the loop.

Now It's Your Turn

1-  In the expanded payroll program in Figure 2-9, identify the first and last statement numbers that form the loop.

_____

_____

*****

There is much branching in this program, but most of it is within the loop.  You should have listed lines 20 and 410.

2-  In Figure 2-9 again, which statement stops the loop?

_____

*****

The "end of data" statement is at line 25: IF S = 0 THEN 500.


SAMPLE PROBLEM

The problem we will solve is to create a 10-year compound interest table showing the year and the balance which has accumulated at the end of each year.  The mathematical formula for compound interest is

$$\text{Balance} = \text{Principal} \times (1 + \text{Interest rate})^{\text{year}}$$

If the principal is $1000, the interest rate is 8%, and the year is 5, the compound interest calculation should be

$$\text{Balance} = 1000 \times (1 + .08)^5$$
$$= 1000 \times (1.08)^5$$
$$= 1000 \times 1.469$$
$$= 1469$$

Observe the order in which these calculations are made. First, the values within the parentheses are added. Second, that answer is raised to the fifth power, exponentiation. And third, the multiplication is performed.

We will use the first three programming steps presented in Chapter 1 to plan the solution to this problem.

1- Study the problem. The input will be the amount of principle and the interest rate. These values will be entered while the program is being run. Part of the output will be a question, "What is the amount of principle and the interest rate?" A heading, COMPOUND INTEREST TABLE, and two column headings, YEAR and BALANCE, will also be printed. A detail line will be printed for each year showing the year and the balance at the end of that year. The process will be to calculate the balance at the end of each year. The loop will be controlled by FOR/NEXT statements.

2- Plan a solution. Figure 3-3 is a program flowchart showing one possible way to solve this problem.

3- Code the computer program. Figure 3-4 is the BASIC program which will produce the compound interest table. Notice that the INPUT statement is used to start the program and that the headings are printed before the loop is started.

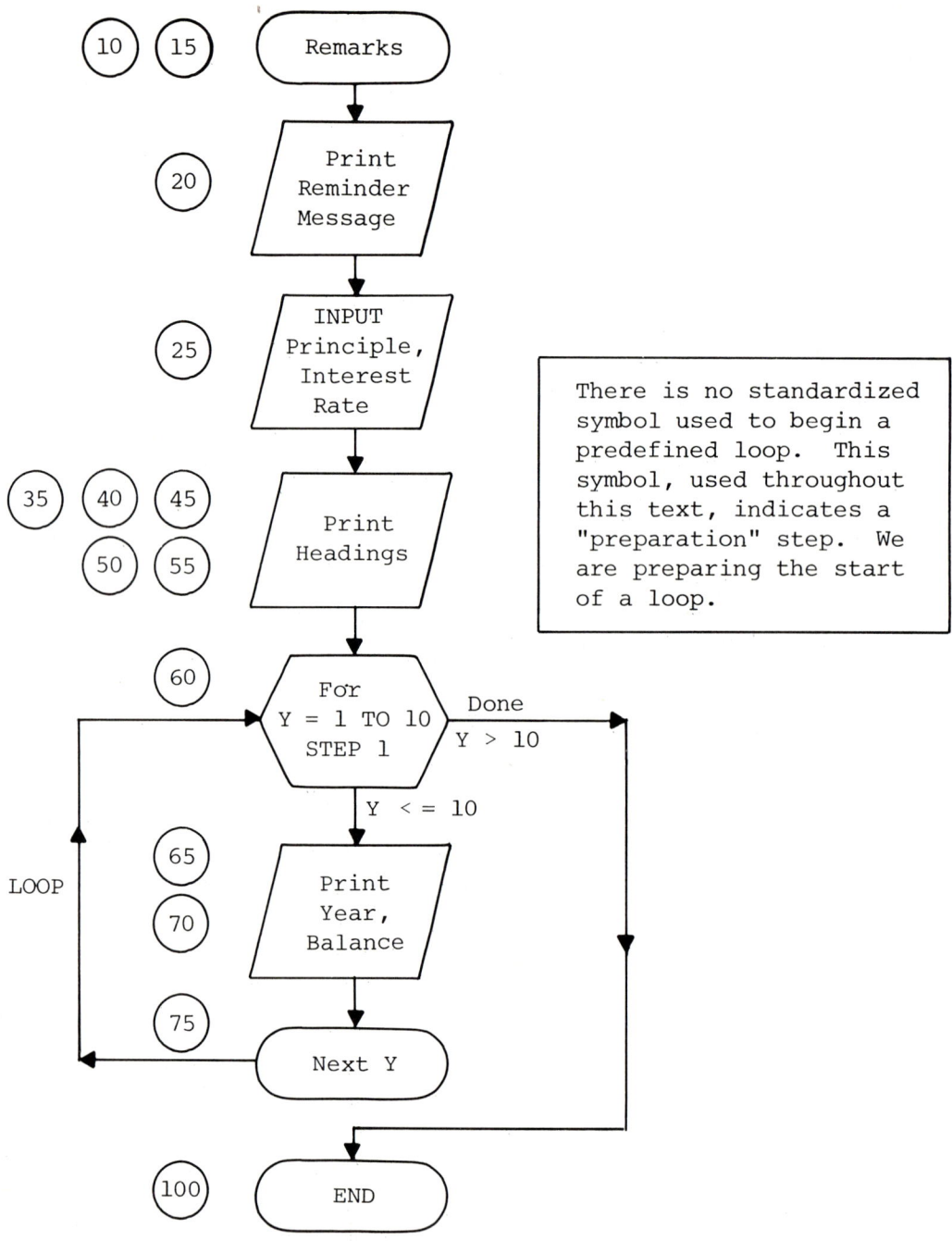

Figure 3-3

Program Flowchart—Compound Interest Table

```
 10   REM   THIS PROGRAM WILL PRINT A 10-YEAR COMPOUND INTEREST TABLE
 15   REM   THE PRINCIPLE AND RATE WILL BE ENTERED DURING EXECUTION
 20   PRINT "WHAT IS THE PRINCIPLE AND INTEREST RATE";
 25   INPUT P, I
 35   PRINT TAB(10); "COMPOUND INTEREST TABLE"
 40   PRINT
 45   PRINT TAB(7); "YEAR"; TAB(30); "BALANCE"
 50   PRINT
 55   PRINT
 60   FOR Y = 1 TO 10 STEP 1
 65   PRINT TAB(9); Y; TAB(30); "$"; P * (1+I)**Y
 70   PRINT
 75   NEXT Y
100   END
```

Figure 3-4

BASIC Program—Compound Interest Table

EXPLANATION OF BASIC STATEMENTS

Before studying the new statements in this program, you should read each statement, study the appropriate flowchart symbol, and make sure you understand those statements that were presented in Chapters 1 and 2. If you have difficulty with lines 10, 15, 20, 35, 45, and 100, please review before you go on.

This BASIC program presents several new statements as well as new uses of statements you have already learned. Line 25, the INPUT statement, shows a new way to enter data. The FOR statement at line 60 and the NEXT statement at line 75 show a new way to form a loop. Also, the PRINT statement at line 65 computes the balance and prints the result. These statements will be discussed in this section.

The INPUT Statement

```
 15   . . .
 20   PRINT "WHAT IS THE PRINCIPLE AND INTEREST RATE";
 25   INPUT P, I
 30   . . .
```

The input statement is most often used with an interactive terminal (teletype or CRT device) and provides a way to enter data into the computer while the program is being executed.

Since you cannot see the program when it is being run, a reminder message should be included in the program. The computer will print the message to tell you what data values should be entered. This is the purpose of line 20. When the program is being executed, the computer will print the following: WHAT IS THE PRINCIPLE AND INTEREST RATE?

Notice the semicolon at the end of line 20. This stops the automatic line spacing on the printer. The computer then executes the INPUT statement at line 25, causing the question mark to be printed right after the reminder message.

---

Remember the "dangling" comma from Chapter 2 which was used to suppress line spacing? This "dangling" semicolon suppresses line spacing and horizontal spacing.

---

The computer will then pause and you will enter the appropriate values. When you push the carriage return key, the computer will accept the data values and continue execution of the program. The INPUT statement at line 25 causes the computer to pause after printing the question mark.

Figure 3-5 shows the computer output from the execution of this program. You can see that the terminal printed the reminder message followed by the question mark. The operator typed "1000, .08" and then pushed the RETURN key. The computer then printed the headings, made the calculations, and printed the values shown.

The INPUT statement is very similar to the READ statement. You make up the variables after INPUT using the same rules for BASIC variables discussed in Chapter 1. The order of the variables should be the same as the order of data values shown in the reminder message so that the user will enter the data correctly. Data are entered in the same way as with a DATA statement, without using the word DATA.

WHAT IS THE PRINCIPLE AND INTEREST RATE ?
    1000,.08


               COMPOUND INTEREST TABLE

        YEAR                    BALANCE

         1                      $ 1080.

         2                      $ 1166.4

         3                      $ 1259.71

         4                      $ 1360.49

         5                      $ 1469.33

         6                      $ 1586.87

         7                      $ 1713.82

         8                      $ 1850.93

         9                      $ 1999.

        10                      $ 2158.92

                    Figure 3-5

        Computer Output—Compound Interest Table


---

In most systems, you may not use the INPUT
statement if you are using a batch terminal or
batch system.  You should use the READ and DATA
statements unless you are working with an
interactive terminal.

---

   As another example of the use of the INPUT statement,
consider a new car dealer.  Assume he has several computer
terminals in his showroom.  A program has been written and
stored.  This program will calculate and print out the amount
of monthly payments to be made by a car buyer.  The salesman
will need to enter the cash price of the auto, the trade-in
value, the interest rate, and the number of months the

contract is to run.  The BASIC statements that will allow
the salesman to enter the needed values are

```
50   PRINT "WHAT IS THE CASH PRICE";
55   INPUT P
60   PRINT "WHAT IS THE TRADE-IN AMOUNT";
65   INPUT T
70   PRINT "WHAT IS THE INTEREST RATE";
75   INPUT I
80   PRINT "HOW MANY MONTHS ON THE CONTRACT"!
85   INPUT M
90   LET . . .
```

These BASIC statements will cause the computer to "ask
for" one data value at a time.  This technique will assure
that the data are entered in the proper order and that the
correct calculations will be made.

     When this program is being run, the terminal will type

     WHAT IS THE CASH PRICE  ?

The carriage will automatically be returned and then pause
while the salesman types the price.  He will then push the
return key.  The terminal will then type

     WHAT IS THE TRADE-IN AMOUNT ?

The salesman will then type in the trade-in allowance and
push the return key.  This interaction between the terminal
and the salesman will continue until the last data value is
entered.  The computer will then continue with the program
(not shown above) to calculate the monthly payments.  The
terminal will then type out an appropriate message and the
amount to be paid each month.

     The general form of the INPUT statement is

| | | |
|---|---|---|
| 1- | Line number | Must precede all BASIC statements. |
| 2- | INPUT | Key word which causes the computer to transfer the data from a terminal to the CPU. |

3-  One or more          Identify CPU storage addresses in
    variables            which data will be stored.  Variables
                         must be made up of one letter or one
                         one letter and one digit.

Now It's Your Turn

1-  Correct the following statement:

    20   INPUT "THE AMOUNT IS";
    21   PRINT A

    _____

    _____

*****

    The two key words are reversed in these statements.  You
should have corrected them as follows:

    20   PRINT "THE AMOUNT IS";
    21   INPUT A

2-  Correct the following statement;

    30   PRINT  TYPE THE NUMBER OF UNITS AND PRICE;
    20   INPUT NP

    _____

    _____

*****

    There are several things wrong.  This is what you should
have written:

    20   PRINT "TYPE THE NUMBER OF UNITS AND PRICE";
    30   INPUT N, P

3-  Code the statement(s) that will allow a terminal user to
enter a customer's charge account number and his outstanding
balance.  Remind the user of the values he is to enter.

    _____

    _____

    _____

    _____

*****

Here are two ways you could have solved this little problem:

```
25   PRINT "WHAT IS THE ACCOUNT NUMBER";
30   INPUT N
35   PRINT "WHAT IS THE BALANCE";
40   INPUT B

25   PRINT "WHAT IS THE ACCOUNT NUMBER AND BALANCE";
30   INPUT N, B
```

## Back to the Sample Program

The PRINT statements in lines 35 through 55 were discussed in Chapter 2. If you are not sure how to use these statements, you should review the explanations in Chapter 2.

## The FOR/NEXT Statements

```
 55   . . .
 60   FOR Y = 1 TO 10 STEP 1
 65   . . .
 70   . . .
 75   NEXT Y
100   . . .
```

Lines 60 and 75 define the loop in this program, an input, process, output loop. The FOR statement at line 60 signals the start of the loop, and the NEXT statement at line 75 indicates the end of the loop. The BASIC statements between the FOR and NEXT statements are executed a number of times as stated in the FOR statement. When the loop is done, gone around ten times, the program branches directly to the statement following the NEXT statement, line 100 in this program.

The FOR statement defines the number of times the loop is to be executed by naming a variable, called the index variable. That variable is given a starting value, a maximum value, and a step or incremental value. In line 60, the index variable is Y, its starting value is 1, the maximum is 10, and the step is 1. This statement tells the computer to loop ten times.

The NEXT statement at line 75 signals the end of the loop. The variable in the NEXT statement must be the same as the index variable used in the FOR statement, Y in this example. The NEXT statement causes the computer to branch back to the

FOR statement with the <u>same</u> index variable. The variable in
the FOR and NEXT statements is the common indicator used by
the computer to form the loop.

FOR/NEXT statements make it easier to program loops.
This problem could have been solved by using two LET
statements, an IF-THEN statement, and a GO TO statement as
follows:

```
57   LET Y = 1
60   IF Y > 10 THEN 100
65   PRINT TAB (9); Y; TAB(30); "$"; P * (1 + I) ** Y
70   PRINT
72   LET Y = Y + 1
75   GO TO 60
100  END
```

In this example, Y is a counter. It is given a starting
value of 1 at line 57 and a maximum value of 10 at line 60.
Y is then given a step value of 1 at line 72. Each time the
program loops from line 60 to line 75, the current value of
Y is compared to 10. As long as Y is less than or equal to
10, the computer continues to line 65 to print the desired
output. The GO TO statement ends the loop. This method is
correct but requires four statements. The FOR/NEXT statements
do the job with only two statements.

Examples of FOR/NEXT Statements

There are several forms and uses of FOR/NEXT statements.
Study these examples carefully. Make sure you can think like
a computer and follow what happens in each example.

Example 1

```
10   FOR J = 1 TO 25 STEP 2
15   PRINT J
20   NEXT J
30   END
```

In this example, the index variable, J, is initially set
(initialized) at 1, is given a maximum value of 25 and a step
value of 2. During the execution of this loop, J will be
equal to 1, 3, 5, 7, ..., 25. The computer will print out the

odd numbers from 1 to 25.  When the loop is done, the computer will branch to line 30 and stop the program.

Example 2

```
50  FOR X = 1 TO 10
.   . . .
70  NEXT X
```

When the STEP is left out, the computer assumes a STEP value of 1.  In this example, X will equal 1, 2, 3, 4, ..., 10.

Example 3

```
10  LET L = 5
20  LET M = 100
30  LET N = 5
40  FOR A = L TO M STEP N
.   . . .
80  NEXT A
```

The index variable A is initialized equal to the value stored in L.  Its maximum value is set equal to the value of M, and the increment is equal to the value of N.  Therefore, A starts at 5 and increases to 100 in steps of 5, as follows: 5, 10, 15, 20, 25, ..., 100.

This example shows that the initialization, maximum, and step values may be variables.  These must be assigned values before the computer gets to the FOR statement.  These values can be assigned with LET statements as shown here, with a READ statement, or with an INPUT statement.

Example 4

```
30  FOR I = .05 TO .08 STEP .01
.   . . .
60  NEXT I
```

The initial, maximum, and step values may be decimal numbers.  You might use this FOR statement in a financial problem in which interest values of 5%, 6%, 7%, and 8% are required.  The index variable, I, will equal .05, .06, .07, and .08.  You may then use I in computing a compound interest table for each interest rate.

Example 5

```
50  FOR N = 10 TO 1 STEP -1
.   . . .
70  NEXT N
```

This FOR statement will cause the index variable, N, to start at 10 and to decrease in value by 1 for each cycle of the loop until N equals 1, as follows:  10, 9, 8, 7, ..., 1.  In some applications, this feature of BASIC is very helpful.

Example 6

```
20  FOR I = 1 TO 5
30  FOR J = 1 TO 3
.   . . .
60  NEXT J
70  NEXT I
```

This example shows that you may place one loop within another, or nest loops.  The J loop, lines 30 to 60, is called the inner loop and is nested within the I loop, which is called the outer loop.  The values of the index variables will be as follows:  When I = 1, J will equal 1, 2, 3;  when I = 2, J will equal 1, 2, 3; when I = 3, J will equal 1, 2, 3; etc.  You should notice that the inner loop goes around three times while the outer loop is at 1; then the inner loop goes around three more times while the outer loop is at 2, and so on until the outer loop has completed its five cycles.

A clock is a good example of nested loops.  The hour hand is the outer loop, and the minute hand is the inner loop. While the hour hand moves from 1:00 to 2:00, the minute hand moves from 1 to 2, from 2 to 3, etc.  In other words, the minute hand goes around from 1 to 12 each time the hour hand changes from 1 to 2, or from 3 to 4, or from 7 to 8.

When you set up nested loops, be sure you do not overlap or cross the loops like this:

```
 ┌─ 20  FOR A = 1 TO 10
 │┌ 30  FOR B = 1 TO 5
 ││ .   . . .
 │└ 60  NEXT A
 └─ 70  NEXT B
```

These loops are not really nested.  If you try this, your
computer will not like it and will not process your program.

Rules for FOR/NEXT Statements

1- Each FOR statement must have its own NEXT statement.
   These statements always come in pairs and must have
   the same index variable.

2- You may leave out the STEP part of the FOR statement.
   The step or incremental value will then be 1.

3- In the FOR statement, the maximum value must be greater
   than the starting value or the loop will not be
   executed (for positive STEP loops).

4- You may include as many statements as you want between
   the FOR and NEXT statements.

5- You must not change the value of the index variable
   or any of the other variables in the FOR statement
   while the loop is being run.  This really confuses
   your computer.

6- You may transfer out of a loop while it is being run
   using an IF-THEN statement.  If the loop is not done,
   you may use the value of the index variable in
   calculations or as output outside the loop.  However,
   you will probably have trouble if you try to transfer
   into the middle of a FOR/NEXT loop.

7- You may use the index variable in any statement
   within the loop as long as you don't change its value.

8- Loops may be nested to almost any depth you want.  The
   number of nested loops allowed depends on the size of
   your computer.  However, be sure you do not cross or
   overlap your loops.

The general form of the FOR statement is

1- Line number     Must precede all BASIC statements.
2- FOR             Key word signaling beginning of a loop.

3-  Variable          Made up by the programmer using the
                      same rules as those for any BASIC
                      variable.  In the FOR statement, this
                      is called the index variable.

4-  =                 Separates the index variable from its
                      starting value, maximum value, and
                      step value.

5-  Constant or       The first character after the equal
    variable          sign sets the starting value of the
                      index variable.

6-  TO                Key word used to separate starting and
                      maximum values of index variable.

7-  Constant or       Sets maximum value of index variable.
    variable

8-  STEP              Key word used to separate maximum and
                      incremental values of index variable.

9-  Constant or       Sets incremental or step value for
    variable          index variable.

The general form of the NEXT statement is

1-  Line number       Required before all BASIC statements.

2-  NEXT              Key word signaling end of loop.

3-  Variable          Must be same as index variable in FOR
                      statement.  Provides the necessary
                      connection between the FOR and the
                      NEXT statements to form the loop.

Now It's Your Turn

1-  Correct any statements that are incorrect:

    20  FOR J < 10 TO 100
    30  . . .
    50  STEP J

    _____

    _____

*****

    You must use an equal sign in line 20 and close the loop
with a NEXT, like this:

    20  FOR J = 10 TO 100
    50  NEXT J

2- Make any necessary corrections in the following statements:

```
 90  LET I = 100
 95  LET K = 5
100  FOR J = I TO 10 STEP K
```

_____

_____

*****

This FOR statement starts J at 100 and decreases it to 10. You need to have a negative STEP, like this:

```
 95  LET K = -5
```

3- Make any corrections necessary in the following statements:

```
200  FOR X = 1 TO 5
210  FOR Y = 1 TO 10 STEP -1
  .    .  .  .
300  NEXT X
310  NEXT Y
```

_____

_____

_____

_____

*****

These loops overlap, and the STEP should be positive.  You should have written

```
210  FOR Y = 1 TO 10 STEP 1
  .    .  .  .
300  NEXT Y
310  NEXT X
```

4- Code the statements that will calculate and print a table of squares and square roots for the digits 1 to 15. Print the digits, their squares, and their square roots. Hint:  Use an index variable that will equal 1, 2, 3, 4, ..., 15.  Also, calculate square roots by raising each digit to the .5 power.

_____

_____

_____

_____

*****

You should have been able to write the following, except
perhaps for line 30:

```
20   FOR X = 1 TO 15
25   LET Y = X ** 2
30   LET Z = X ** .5     (this calculates the square root of X)
35   PRINT X, Y, Z
40   NEXT X
```

Back to the Sample Program—The PRINT Statement Revisited

```
55   . . .
60   FOR Y
65   PRINT TAB(9); Y; TAB(30); "$": P * (1 + I) ** Y
70   PRINT
75   . . .
```

Here is still another version of the PRINT statement.  You
are familiar with the TAB function and the "$".  But what
happens when an arithmetic expression, P * (1 + I) ** Y, is
included as in line 65?

The computer calculates the answer and then prints it for
you.  In this example, the computer will calculate the amount
of the balance for year Y and print that amount as shown in
Figure 3-5.

You should notice that the index variable, Y, is used in
this PRINT statement.  This is an example of Rule 7 on
FOR/NEXT statements.  You can see that the value of Y is
printed to indicate the year.  Y is also used in the compound
interest calculation as the exponent.  In both cases, the
value of the index variable is not changed.  This is a correct
use of the index variable in a statement within the loop.

Let's look at another example of an arithmetic expression
as part of a PRINT statement:

```
100  LET X = 5.7
120  PRINT X - 2, 3 * X
150  END
```

This little program will print two answers, 3.7 and 17.1.
However, you won't be able to calculate the sum of these two
answers and print the answer unless you write a BASIC statement as follows:

```
130  PRINT (X - 2) + (3 * X)
```

In other words, the answers calculated in the PRINT statement
at line 120 are not saved by the computer and cannot be used
in later statements.

You should notice that the PRINT statement includes only
an arithmetic expression, not an arithmetic statement.  The
following PRINT statement would not be correct because it
includes an arithmetic statement:

        200  PRINT X, Y, Z = X * Y

This statement will keep the computer from executing the
program because of the arithmetic statement, Z = X * Y.  If
you want to print out the values X, Y and their product,
your PRINT statement should look like this:

        200  PRINT X, Y, X * Y

However, if you want to use the product of X and Y later
in your program, you should code the following statements:

        190  LET Z = X * Y
        200  PRINT X, Y, Z
        .   . . .
        300  LET A = Z / 3.14

The general form of the PRINT statement for calculation
is

| | | |
|---|---|---|
| 1- | Line number | Required for all BASIC statements. |
| 2- | PRINT | Key word which activates the output device. |
| 3- | Arithmetic expression | Any expression that is valid in BASIC. Must not include a variable followed by an equal sign. |

Now It's Your Turn

Correct the statements in Exercises 1 and 2.  Assume that
values have already been assigned to all variables.

1-  25  PRINT "THE AVERAGE IS", A = N / C

_____

*****

You should remember that your computer will not accept
the A = in a PRINT statement.  You should have written

    25  PRINT "THE AVERAGE IS", N / C

2-  30  PRINT A + B, C + D
    31  PRINT "THE SUM OF A + B AND C + D IS", X

_____

_____

*****

    Remember, the computer does not save the answers calculated
in PRINT statements.

    30  OK AS IS
    31  PRINT "THE SUM OF A+B AND C+D IS", (A + B) + (C + D)

3-  Code a statement that will print the message THE PRESENT
BALANCE IS; then calculate the present balance = old balance +
purchases - payments, and print the answer.

    50 _____
*****

    This should have been easy for you, but remember, you
cannot include a complete arithmetic statement in a PRINT:

    50  PRINT "THE PRESENT BALANCE IS", O + P - A

## Back to the Sample Program

    The NEXT Y statement at line 75 will close the loop and
cause the computer to return to the FOR statement at line 60.
The loop will continue until it has cycled ten times.  The
program then stops with the END statement at line 100.

## Summary of New Statements in Sample Program

    1-  The INPUT statement is used to enter data while the
        program is being executed.  The computer will
        execute the INPUT statement, print a question mark
        on the terminal, and pause.  The user will then enter
        the needed data on the terminal and press the return

key.  The computer will then continue with its
execution of the program using the data just entered.

2-  FOR/NEXT statements are used to define one or more
    loops within a program.  The FOR and NEXT statements
    are tied together by the same index variable.  The
    FOR statement gives the beginning, maximum, and
    step values for the index variable.  These values tell
    the computer how many times the loop should be executed.

3-  The PRINT statement may be used to make arithmetic
    calculations and print the resulting answer.  You
    must be careful to include an expression only, not
    an arithmetic statement.  Never include an equal sign.


NOW IT'S YOUR TURN PROBLEM—COMPOUND INTEREST TABLE

Your problem is to cause the computer to print a compound
interest table for a principle of $1.00 at 5%, 6%, 7%, 8%,
and 9% interest for 10 years.  You will solve this problem
using nested FOR/NEXT loops and the calculating PRINT statement.
Figure 3-6 is the program flowchart for planning your solution.

Your job now is to write the BASIC statements that will
solve this problem.  Study the program flowchart and the
suggestions.  Then write the BASIC statement or statements
that are represented by the flowchart symbol.  After you have
written your statement, check it against my suggested
statement.  If you didn't get it right, go back in the·chapter
and review the material.

Lines 10, 11:  These should identify the program and the
programmer.

    10 _____
    11 _____
*****

    10  REMARK COMPOUND INTEREST TABLE - 5%, 6%, 7%, 8%, 9% INTEREST
    11  REM M. ANDERSON

Remember, the REMARK statement is used to explain the program

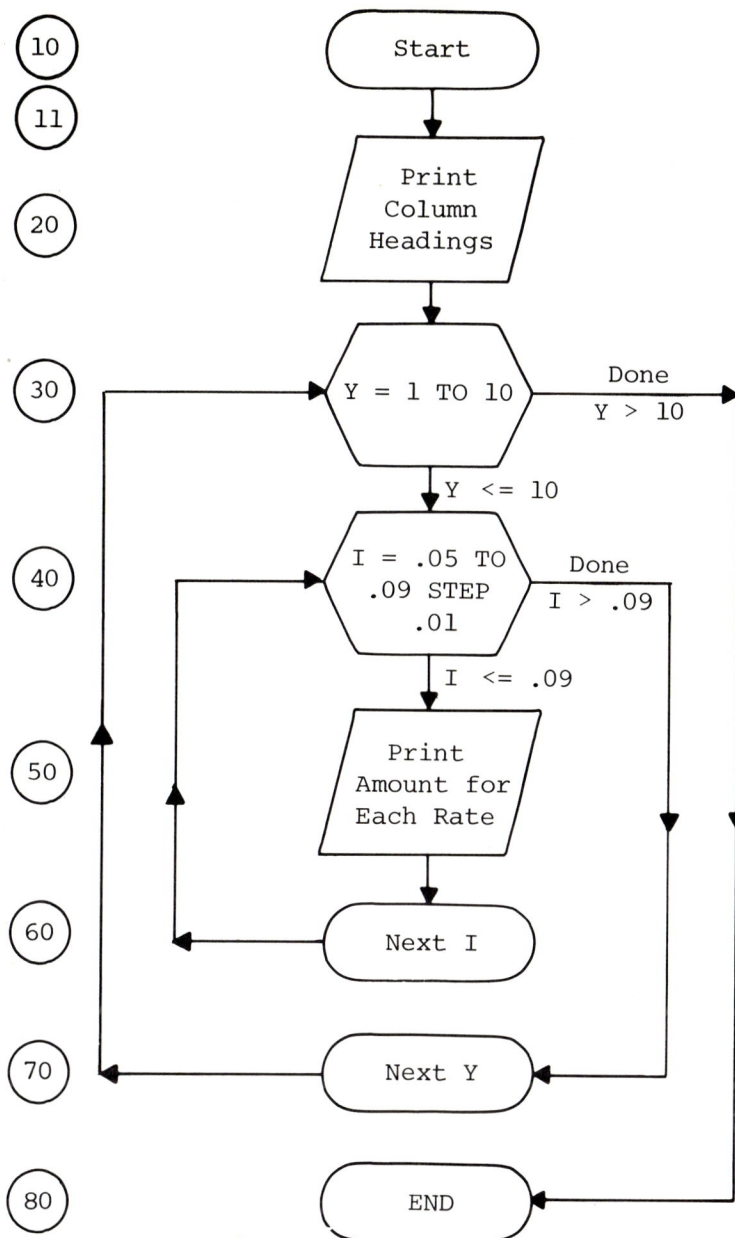

Figure 3-6

Program Flowchart—Compound Interest Table

or some part of it.  These statements have no effect on the program.

<u>Line 20</u>:  You should print out the following column headings:

    5 PERCENT    6 PERCENT    7 PERCENT    8 PERCENT    9 PERCENT

    20 _____

*****

Here is what you should have written:

```
20  PRINT   "5 PERCENT", "6 PERCENT", "7 PERCENT", "8 PERCENT", "9 PERCENT"
```

You want to make sure that your headings are printed before you get into a loop. Also, since you want to print headings for five columns, you may as well use the automatic spacing feature by separating each heading with a comma.

Line 30:  In this problem, we want to calculate and print 10 detail lines.  Line 30 should set up a loop to do this.

    30 _____
*****

One way you could have coded the beginning of this loop is

```
30  FOR Y = 1 TO 10
```

We don't need the STEP because we want to print and calculate for the years 1 through 10.  I used Y as my index variable since it represents "years."

Line 40:  Watch out for this one.  Maybe you should look back at FOR/NEXT Example 5 before you try this one.  We want to calculate five compound interest amounts for each year.  The easiest way to do this is to set up an inner loop so that the index variable I (interest) will equal the five different percent values stated in the problem.  Try it.

    40 _____
*****

Does yours look like this?

```
40  FOR I = .05 TO .09 STEP .01
```

I hope you remembered to convert 5% to .05, etc.  If you wrote

```
40  FOR I = 5 TO 9 STEP 1
```

you can still correct your arithmetic in line 50.  Can you?

<u>Line 50</u>:  This statement should cause the computer to print
five values, the balance at 5%, the balance at 6%, etc.
Watch this one or you will have everything printing in one
column, not across the page under the column headings.  Also,
you will want to use the index variables Y and I in your
calculations.

    50 _____

*****

I would code this statement like this:

   50  PRINT (1 + I) ** Y,

If you did not end your PRINT statement with a comma, each of
the five amounts for the first year will be printed in a
column in the first print zone.  Your computer would repeat
this for each of the 10 years, 50 lines of print!

When you include the index variable, I, in your
arithmetic expression, you tell the computer to make compound
interest calculations for interest rates of .05, .06, .07, .08,
and .09 all this while the index variable, Y, equals 1.  The
computer then repeats these calculations while Y equals 2,
repeats again while Y equals 3, and so on until Y equals 10.
The computer, therefore, makes <u>50</u> compound interest
calculations, 5 for each year.  But remember, do not put an
equal sign in a PRINT statement.

<u>Line 60</u>:  You want a statement that will end the inner loop.

    60 _____

*****

Here is the only correct statement you could have entered:

   60  NEXT I

Be sure you use the correct index variable here because your
computer does not like crossed loops.  Also, when you start
a loop with a FOR statement as you did at line 40, you must
end that loop with a NEXT statement.

<u>Line 70</u>:  This should be easy.  You need to end the outer
loop.

   70 _____
*****

   There is only one correct way to do this one, right?

   70  NEXT Y

<u>Line 80</u>:  You need to tell your computer that your program
is completed.

   80 _____
*****

   If you missed this one, return to Chapter 1, do not pass
GO, do not collect $200.

   Your completed BASIC program should read like this one:

```
10   REMARK COMPOUND INTEREST TABLE - 5%, 6%, 7%, 8%, 9%, INTEREST
11   REM M. ANDERSON
20   PRINT "5 PERCENT", "6 PERCENT", "7 PERCENT", "8 PERCENT", "9 PERCENT"
30   FOR Y = 1 TO 10
40   FOR I = .05 TO .09 STEP .01
50   PRINT (1 + I) ** Y,
60   NEXT I
70   NEXT Y
80   END
```

SUMMARY

   In this chapter, you have learned about program loops,
particularly predefined loops using FOR and NEXT statements.
Two types of loops were discussed, the input, process, output
loop and the input, process loop.  Most business data
processing applications use the first type.

   The new BASIC statements that you learned are

   1-  INPUT              Provides a method of entering
                          data into computer system while
                          program is being executed.

      <u>line number</u>  <u>INPUT</u>  <u>numeric or string variable(s)</u>

2-  FOR                    Defines the start of a loop.
                           Names an index variable, assigns
                           a beginning, maximum, and step
                           value to index variable.

    line number   FOR    index variable  beginning value  TO

    maximum value  STEP  incremental value

3-  NEXT                   Ends loop.  Used only with FOR
                           statement.  Must use same index
                           variable as FOR statement.

    line number   NEXT   index variable

4-  PRINT                  May be used to calculate and print
                           an answer.  Must not include
                           complete arithmetic statement.

    line number   PRINT  arithmetic expression


EXERCISES

A-  Draw a loop flowchart (i.e., Figure 3-1 or 3-2) for the
grocery check-out system presented in Chapter 1.

B-  Code a FOR and NEXT statement for each of the following:

  1-  To process 60 data values for statistical analysis.
  2-  To vary the index variable from 1 to 25 by
      increments of .5.

C-  Assume the number of values in a statistical sample, N,
has been stored in the CPU.  Code the FOR and NEXT statements
to process these data.

D-  The formula for the length of a hypotenuse, h, of a right
triangle is $h = \sqrt{a^2 + b^2}$, where a and b are the two sides of the
triangle.  Code a BASIC statement that will output the message
"The length of the hypotenuse is" followed by the calculated
value of h.

E-  Make any needed corrections in the following independent
BASIC statements; do not make unnecessary corrections:

  1-   27 FOR NUM = 1, 16, 3

```
2-     30 FOR M3 = M1 TO M

3-     41 READ A, C, 2.95, DOE, X, Y, Z N, J, M

4-     60 FOR N = 10 TO STEP 1

5-    300 PRINT X, Y, 3.1417R

6-     30 FOR Y = 1 TO 100
          . . . .
        5 NEXT Y

7-     10 IF A = B THEN 20
       20 PRINT A * B, "THIS IS THE PRODUCT"

8-     40 FOR Z = 10 TO X STEP 10
          . . . .
      120 NEXT X

9-     32 FOR A = 1 TO 15
       33 PRINT
       34 NEXT A
```

PROBLEMS

1-  Business managers frequently need to know the present
value of an investment at varying rates of interest for
varying lengths of time.  In other words, how many cents must
be invested today (present value) to produce $1 10 years
from now if invested at 5% interest?

 Code a BASIC program to create a present value table for
$1 for each of 10 years at interest rates of 4%, 6%, 8%, and
10%.  The formula for the present value, p, is

$$p = 1(1 + r)^{-y} = \frac{1}{1(1 + r)y}$$

where r = interest rate and y = year.

 The output should consist of five column headings as
follows:

|      | FOUR    | SIX     | EIGHT   | TEN     |
|------|---------|---------|---------|---------|
| YEAR | PERCENT | PERCENT | PERCENT | PERCENT |

There should then be ten lines following the column headings,
one for each year, showing the year and the present values for
the four interest rates at the end of the year.

2- Two often-used statistics in business are the mean (average) and standard deviation. The mean is a number that represents some aspect of a group. For instance, the mean annual income for a group of people in a neighborhood will help a marketing manager decide whether or not to open a store selling luxury items.

The standard deviation is a measure of dispersion and will tell us how varied the data are. The larger the standard deviation, the more varied are the data.

The formula for the mean is

$$\frac{\Sigma X}{N}$$

$\Sigma$ is the Greek letter sigma and means "sum of." You will need to accumulate or add up all the values of X.

The formula for the standard deviation is

$$\sqrt{\frac{\Sigma X^2 - (\Sigma X)^2/N}{N-1}}$$

The $\Sigma X^2$ is different from $(\Sigma X)^2$. Study the following table:

| X | $X^2$ |
|---|---|
| 2 | 4 |
| 3 | 9 |
| 1 | 1 |
| 4 | 16 |
| $\Sigma X = 10$ | $\Sigma X^2 = 30$ |

If we square $\Sigma X$, which is the same as $(\Sigma X)^2$, we get an answer of 100, while the $\Sigma X^2$ equals only 30.

| | |
|---|---|
| Output | An appropriate message, the mean. |
| | An appropriate message, the standard deviation. |
| Input | One data value, the value of N. |
| | N data elements, values of X. |
| Processes | Accumulate values of X. |
| | Accumulate values of $X^2$. |
| | Calculate mean. |
| | Calculate standard deviation. |
| Transfer | Control loop(s) using FOR/NEXT statements. |
| Test data | 20, 45, 56, 43, 61, 57, 60, 49, 55, 62, 58, |
| | 48, 51, 58, 64, 59, 64, 56, 47, 44, 61 |

3-   An important computation for certain types of probability
is the number of ways r objects may be selected from among n
objects.   This is called the number of combinations of n
things taken r at a time.   The formula for the number of
combinations, C, is

$$C = \frac{n!}{r!(n - r)!}$$

(n! is called n factorial.   When n = 5, n! = 1 x 2 x 3 x 4 x
5 = 120.)

Write a BASIC program to calculate the number of
combinations of n things taken r at a time.   If you are using
an interactive terminal, use INPUT for n and r with an
appropriate reminder message.   You should keep the value of n
less than or equal to 10.   If you are using a batch system,
make n = 10 and r = 3.   The output should include an
appropriate message showing the values of n and r and the
value of C.   Use three separate FOR/NEXT loops to compute C.

# 4

# One-Dimensional Arrays—Lists

INTRODUCTION

In our programming up to this time, we have used only a few
data values at any one time.  We have read and stored two or
three data values, processed those values, produced some
output, then repeated these steps over and over again until
all the data have been processed.  For many business
applications, this procedure does the job for us.

But in many other applications, we will want to read and
store many data values, to reuse these data values several
times within a program, and perhaps to change these values.

Fortunately, BASIC gives a neat, simple way to process
many data values by using lists and tables, or arrays.  A
list is a one-dimensional array, and a table is a two-
dimensional array.

After you have mastered this chapter you will be able to

1- Store data in a list using a FOR/NEXT loop.
2- Accumulate data in a list using data elements input
   from a transaction.
3- Search through the values in a list to find the one
   that helps solve the problem.
4- Search through the values in a list to find and save
   the largest of those values.
5- Use values stored in a list to make calculations.
6- Print values stored in a list.

But first, we should learn some of the main ideas about
arrays in general.

125

PROGRAMMING CONCEPTS

Many business programming jobs are made much simpler by
using one or more arrays.  For example, the median (statistics)
is a measure of central tendency and is defined as the data
value found at the middle of a set of data when those data are
arranged in ascending or descending order.  Usually data are
not prearranged before they are entered into the computer.
Therefore, we must read these data into a one-dimensional
array, or list, then sort them before we can find the median.

Another example will help you understand the importance
of arrays.  There are 100 different items in our inventory.
We want to make sure we keep an accurate count of each item by
subtracting all those items sold from inventory and adding
all items received.  One way to do this is to store the
identification number and the number on hand for each of the
100 items in a two-dimensional array or table.  Whenever we
make a sale, we  can look up the ID number in our table and
then subtract the number of items sold from the quantity on
hand, stored in the table.  Tables will be discussed in
Chapter 5.

What Is a List?

A list can be thought of as a post office in a small
town.  In this post office, there are many post office boxes,
each of which has a number.  If we want to send a letter to a
friend in this small town, we will address the letter

                    John Anderson
                    Box 32
                    Summitville, Colorado

All the post office boxes in Summitville have different
numbers, perhaps ranging from Box 1 to Box 300.  But all the
boxes have the same name, Summitville.  John's address may be
thought of as Summitville, Box 32.  Or we could simplify his
address to Summitville (32).  The bank's address may be
Summitville, Box 2, or Summitville (2).

A list is a group of storage cells (post office boxes)

each of which has a different number but which has the same
name.  We use a list to store many data elements of the same
kind, such as many different prices.  Suppose that we name our
list with the variable X (a town named X) and also that we
have only ten storage cells in our list.  List X will look
like this:

List X

| 1 | 2 | 3 | 4 | 5 | 6 | 7 | 8 | 9 | 10 | |
|---|---|---|---|---|---|---|---|---|----|---|
|   |   |   |   |   |   |   |   |   |    |   |

Notice that all the cells have only one name, X, but that
each has a different number.  If we want to refer to the first
cell in X, we use the address X(1) (read "X sub one").  X(10),
read "X sub 10," is the address of the last cell in the list.
We can store 5.27 in cell 3 of the X list like this:

        25  LET X(3) = 5.27

Or we can code it this way:

        35  READ X(3)
        36  DATA 5.27

After either line 25 or line 35 is executed, list X will look
like this:

List X

| 1 | 2 | 3 | 4 | 5 | 6 | 7 | 8 | 9 | 10 | |
|---|---|------|---|---|---|---|---|---|----|---|
|   |   | 5.27 |   |   |   |   |   |   |    |   |

In these examples, the number in the parentheses is
called a subscript, and the variable name plus its subscript
is called a subscripted variable.  The combination of the
list name and a subscript identifies a specific storage cell
within that list.  For instance, X(5) identifies storage cell
number 5 in list X.  A subscript may be a number, a variable,
or an expression.  If K = 5, X(K) refers to cell number 5 in
list X.  If K = 5, X(K - 2) refers to cell number 3 in list X.

### Storing Data in a List

Suppose we want to read and store ten values into list X.
We could code a program segment as follows:

```
20  READ X(1), X(2), X(3), X(4), X(5), X(6), X(7), X(8), X(9), X(10)
30  DATA 22, 13, 41, 12, 27, 32, 19, 20, 31, 45
```

This approach is correct. But what if you wanted to store
100 data values? I am sure you agree that it would be very
inefficient to use this method. Let's try a different approach.
We will use a FOR/NEXT loop and use the index variable as the
subscript in the READ statement, like this:

```
15  FOR N = 1 TO 10
20  READ X(N)
25  NEXT N
30  DATA 22, 13, 41, 12, 27, 32, 19, 20, 31, 45
```

In this FOR/NEXT loop, the index variable N will equal 1, 2,
3, ..., 10. Therefore, when the READ statement is executed
the first time, N will equal 1, and the first data value will
be stored in X(1). Then N will equal 2, and the second data
value will be stored in X(2). When the loop is done, the
list X will look like this:

List X

| 1 | 2 | 3 | 4 | 5 | 6 | 7 | 8 | 9 | 10 |
|----|----|----|----|----|----|----|----|----|----|
| 22 | 13 | 41 | 12 | 27 | 32 | 19 | 20 | 31 | 45 |

Notice carefully the two variables used in this program
segment. The index variable in the FOR/NEXT statements is N.
The variable X is used to name the list, and the index variable
is used to identify each specific storage cell in list X. Your
computer will take a dim view of your programming skill if you
wrote

```
15  FOR X = 1 TO 10
20  READ X(X)
25  NEXT X
```

Now, if we want to read and store 100 data values, all we

need to do is make our FOR/NEXT loop cycle 100 times.  And,
of course, we need to provide 100 data values.

You should notice that storage cells in lists are just like
other storage positions in BASIC.  The only difference is the
position name or address.  The address of a storage in a list
is a <u>subscripted variable</u>, and the address of any other storage
position is a <u>simple variable</u> or a <u>string variable</u>.

You have seen that we can READ or INPUT values into a list.
When we do this, we erase any old values and store new values
in their place.  We can PRINT values from a list without
losing the values.  We can calculate values into a list using
the LET statement.  This erases the old value and stores a
new value.  And, finally, we can use list values in an
expression to the right of an equal sign in the LET statement.
These list values are not changed.

<u>Now It's Your Turn</u>

1- Code a program segment that will read and store 15 data
elements into list Z.  Assume the data values are provided.

```
10  DATA . . .

20 _____
30 _____
40 _____
```
*****

```
10  DATA . . .
20  FOR N = 1 TO 15
30    READ Z(N)
40  NEXT N
```

You could have used a different index variable in your FOR/
NEXT statements from that shown above.  You could have
included STEP 1 in your FOR statement.  <u>But</u> if your answer
was different in any other way, you goofed.  Notice that the
index variable, N, <u>must</u>  be used as the subscript in the
READ statement and that you must READ the data values into
list Z.

2-  Code a program segment that will square the integers from 1 to 25 and store those answers in list P.  (Hint:  You will not need any data.)

```
10 _____
20 _____
30 _____
```
*****

Your three lines should look like this:

```
10  FOR X = 1 TO 25
20  LET P(X) = X ** 2
30  NEXT X
```

Act like a computer and think this one through.  Notice that we used the index variables for the subscript <u>and</u> for the calculations.  However, we did not change the value of X within the loop.

SAMPLE PROBLEM

The problem we are going to solve is to create an invoice register.  We will read in data about a credit sale, which will include the customer's name, the product identification number, and the number of units purchased.  We will then search through a product ID number list to find the right product, then use the price from the price list to calculate the amount of the invoice.

The first type of input will be the product-price data for 20 products and will include a product ID number and the price per unit.  The second type of input will be data for each sale, which will include the customer's name, the product ID number, and the number of units sold.

The output will be a report with the following column headings:

NAME       PRODUCT ID      UNITS      PRICE      AMOUNT

There will be also one detail line printed for each transaction (sale) to include the customer's name, the product identification number, the number of units sold, the price of that product, and the amount of the invoice.

There will be only one calculation in this program, amount = units x price.  We will have to make a last data decision and a product ID decision.  One FOR/NEXT loop will be needed to read and store the product and price data in two one-dimensional lists.  We will need a second FOR/NEXT loop to search through the product ID number list to find the right product.

Figure 4-1 is a program flowchart showing the solution plan, and Figure 4-2 is the BASIC program.

Remember, on some computer systems, alphabetic data must be enclosed in quotes in the DATA statement.  On other systems, the string variable, C$, must be dimensioned in the DIM statement.  Still other systems require both of these.  Check the specifications for your computer system.

EXPLANATION OF BASIC STATEMENTS

This BASIC program has several sections.  Lines 100 through 130 store the product identification (ID) numbers in list N and the unit prices in list P.  Lines 300 through 310 search through the product ID number list until the ID number in the transaction is equal to one of the numbers in the ID number list.  When this occurs, the computer branches out of the FOR/NEXT loop to line 400.  The amount of the purchase is calculated at line 410; the detail line is printed. The program then branches back to read the next transaction.

If no equal condition is found, the program completes the FOR/NEXT loop and continues to line 320, which prints out an error message, and then returns to read the next transaction.

Please refer to Figure 4-2 while you study the following paragraph.

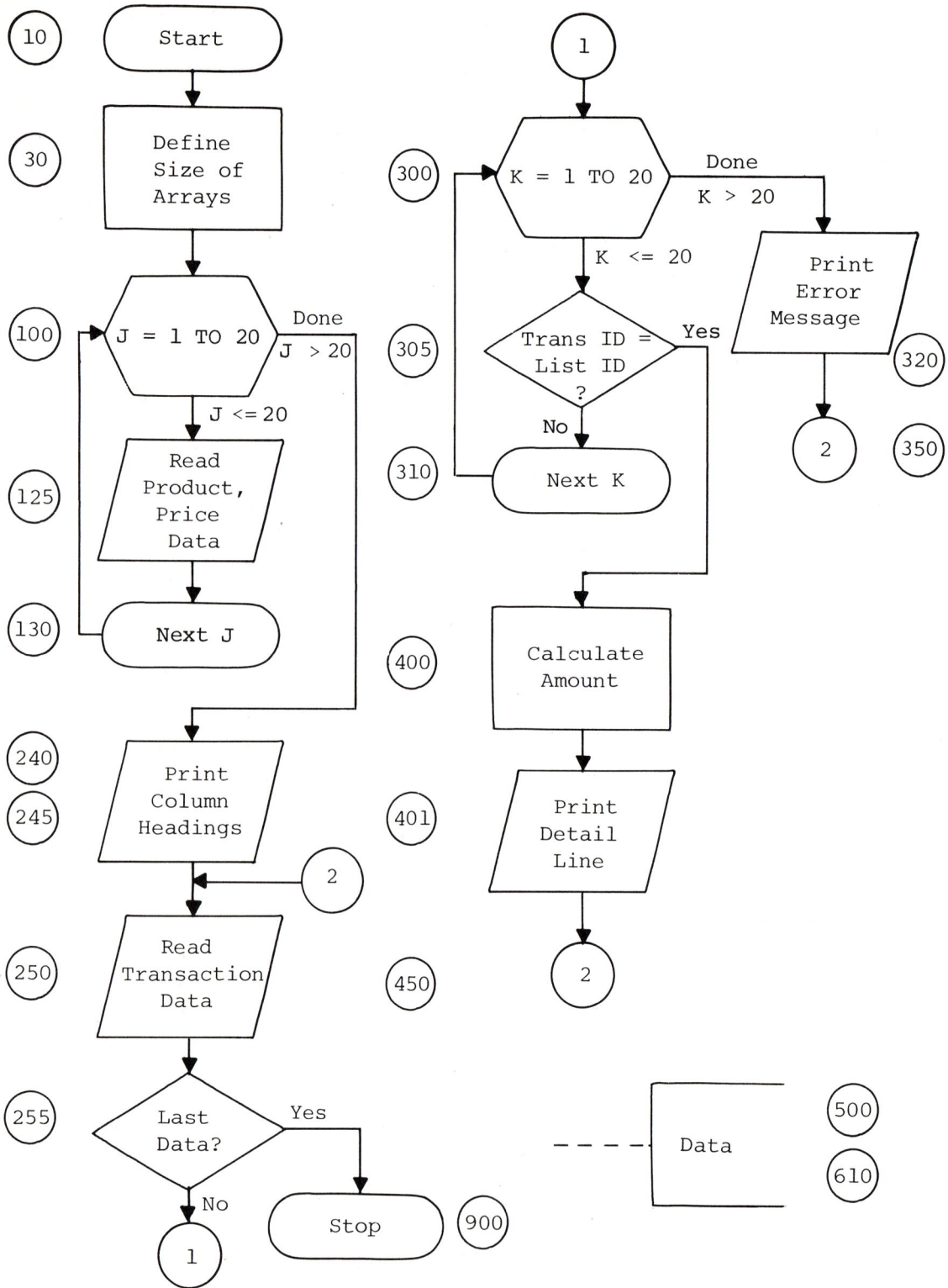

Figure 4-1

Program Flowchart—Invoice Register

132

```
 10   REM INVOICE REGISTER
 30   DIM N(20), P(20)
100   FOR J = 1 TO 20
125   READ N(J), P(J)
130   NEXT J
240   PRINT 'NAME', 'PRODUCT ID', 'UNITS', 'PRICE', 'AMOUNT'
245   PRINT
250   READ C$, I, U
255   IF I = 0 THEN 900
300   FOR K = 1 TO 20
305   IF I = N(K) THEN 400
310   NEXT K
320   PRINT 'INPUT ERROR FOR'; C$
350   GO TO 250
400   LET A = P(K) * U
410   PRINT C$, N(K), U, P(K), A
450   GO TO 250
500   DATA 123, 4.50, 128, 1.25, 130, 6.08, 143, 10.50
501   DATA 150, 2.25, 152, 3.89, 154, 1.95, 158, 2.05
502   DATA 161, 3.80, 164, 7.21, 165, 6.49, 167, 12.50
503   DATA 171, .45, 175, 2.10, 177, 5.20, 179, 3.40
505   DATA 190, 3.00, 195, 4.52, 196, 7.08, 199, 1.60
600   DATA JANE ADAMS, 130, 100
601   DATA BOB AARON, 167, 10
602   DATA BILL QUINCY, 128, 50
603   DATA FRED HUBERT, 667, 50
604   DATA HELEN GONE, 175, 12
605   DATA NANCY HOBBS, 152, 25
610   DATA ALL DONE, 0, 0
900   END
```

Figure 4-2

BASIC Program—Invoice Register

There are several new BASIC statements in this program. All of these apply to the product ID number and price lists. Line 30 defines the size of the two lists, and line 125 stores the data into these lists. At line 305, the ID number in the transaction is compared to each number in list N. Line 400 uses the appropriate value from the unit price list to calculate the amount of the purchase. The number and the price from the two lists are included in the printed detail line at line 410.

The DIM Statement

```
 10   . . .
 30   DIM N(20), P(20)
100   . . .
```

The DIM statement (short for DIMension) at line 30 defines the two lists. This statement tells the computer to set aside 20 CPU storage positions for list N, which will hold the product ID number. The statement also directs the computer to set aside 20 storage cells for list P, which will hold the product prices.

The DIM statement defines the maximum number of data elements that may be stored in a list. In this example, no more than 20 elements may be stored in list N or in list P. But we do not have to use all 20 storage cells. We could use only 10 of them. If there were 100 items in our inventory, we would need to change our DIM statement to

     21  DIM N(100), P(100)

If your program requires several lists of different sizes, you may define these in one DIM statement as follows:

     512  DIM A(25), X(1000), C(5)

In this example, three lists are defined: A with 25 positions, X with 1000, and C with only 5. You can see that the size of each list is specified with whole numbers enclosed in parentheses. You may not use a variable or an arithmetic expression to define the size of a list.

The general form of the DIM statement is

| | | |
|---|---|---|
| 1- | Line number | Must precede all BASIC statements. |
| 2- | DIM | Key word telling computer to set aside storage positions for a list. |
| 3- | List name | A simple variable (alphabetic character) used to identify the list. |
| 4- | List size | Whole number enclosed in parentheses; specifies the maximum number of storage cells in the list. |

Now It's Your Turn

The following DIM statements are incorrect. Explain why, and make any needed corrections.

1-    31   DIM X(N + 30)

_____

_____

*****

A DIM statement may not include an arithmetic expression.
You should have written something like this:

      31   DIM X(130)

2-    41   LET N = 20
      42   DIM Z(N)

_____

_____

*****

A DIM statement may not include a variable within the
parentheses, even when the variable has been previously
defined as in line 41 above.  You should have defined list
Z like this:

      42   DIM Z(20)

3-    51   DIM Q 35

_____

*****

The size of the list, 35 in this example, must be
enclosed in parentheses.  Your corrected DIM statement should
have looked like this:

      51   DIM (35)

4-   Write the statement(s) that will define three lists with
100, 25, and 50 storage positions.  The lists are to be
named A, B, and C.

_____

_____

_____

*****

I hope you didn't let the three answer lines fool you. You only needed one DIM statement, like this:

```
112  DIM A(100), B(25), C(50)
```

Three DIM statements are correct and will work, but that is not efficient programming.

## Storing Data in Lists

```
 30  . . .
100  FOR J = 1 TO 20
125  READ N(J), P(J)
130  NEXT J
240  . . .
      .
```

Lines 100, 125, and 130 read and store 20 data elements in list N and 20 data elements in list P. You should remember that we can use the index variable, J, as a subscript. When we do this, the subscript for list N and list P will vary from 1 to 20, causing the first data element from line 500 to be stored in N(1) and the second in P(1).

After the first execution of the READ statement, lists N and P will look like this:

List N

| 1 | 2 | 3 | ... | 20 |
|---|---|---|-----|----|
| 123 | | | ... | |

List P

| 1 | 2 | 3 | ... | 20 |
|---|---|---|-----|----|
| 4.50 | | | ... | |

The FOR statement at line 100 will now cause J to equal 2. The third data element will be stored in N(2), and the fourth element will be stored in P(2) as follows:

List N

| 1 | 2 | 3 | ... | 20 |
|---|---|---|-----|----|
| 123 | 128 | | ... | |

List P

| 1 | 2 | 3 | ... | 20 |
|---|---|---|-----|----|
| 4.50 | 1.25 | | ... | |

This loop will continue until 20 ID numbers are stored in list N and 20 unit prices are stored in list P.

There are several important ideas that you should remember when you store data into lists and tables.

1- The arrangement of the data in the DATA statements dictates the way you code your FOR/NEXT and READ statements. In the sample program, the data are arranged in pairs: an ID number and a price for each product. If the data were arranged so that the first 20 data elements were the 20 product ID numbers and the next 20 elements were the unit prices, the FOR/NEXT and READ statements would have to be changed.

2- The variable used as the subscript in the READ statement is the index variable from the FOR statement. In the sample program, J is the index variable, and J is also the subscript for list N and list P. The following program segment will **not** store the desired data in the two lists.

```
100   FOR X = 1 TO 20
105   READ N(J), P(J)
125   NEXT X
```

In most computer systems, the subscript J will equal zero. The computer will execute the READ statement 20 times and will try to store 20 data elements in N(0) and 20 in P(0). If you want to use X as the index variable in the FOR statement, then you must use X as subscript in the READ statement.

3- The maximum size that the index variable may reach must not be greater than the size of the list as defined in the DIM statement. The two lists in the sample program were given a maximum size of 20 in the DIM statement, and the maximum value of the index variable was set at 20 in the FOR statement. The following segment would not "run":

```
100   DIM Z(25)
200   FOR J = 1 TO 100
250   READ Z(J)
300   NEXT J
```

The computer will store data in Z(1) to Z(25).  But
when J reaches 26, the computer will try to store
data in Z(26).  The computer has been told that there
are only 25 storage cells in list Z; therefore Z(26)
does not exist.  The computer will stop and print an
error message.

### Now It's Your Turn

Correct any errors you find in Exercises 1, 2, and 3.

```
1-      5   DIM Q(30)
       10   FOR Q = 1 TO 30
       15   READ Z(Q)
       20   NEXT Z
      100   DATA . . .
```

_____

_____

_____

*****

Watch this one.  This is a case of mixed-up variables.
Your corrections should be something like this:

```
    5   DIM Z(30)          10   FOR Z = 1 TO 30
    .   . . .        or    15   READ Q(Z)
   20   NEXT Q
```

2- This program segment is designed to store 50 data
elements into list A.

```
   50   DIM A(20)
   60   FOR X = 1 TO 50
   70   NEXT X
   80   READ X(A)
```

_____

_____

_____

*****

Your corrections must be

```
   50   DIM A(50)
   60   . . .
   70   READ A(X)
   80   NEXT X
```

I hope you placed the READ statement within the FOR/NEXT loop.
If you didn't, nothing would be read into the list.

Be sure you use <u>different</u> variables for your index variable and list name.  Don't confuse your computer.  Also, use the <u>same</u> list name in your READ statement as you used in your DIM.  Don't you be dim!

3- This program segment is designed to store 30 data elements into list C.

```
20   DIM C(30)
30   LET I = 1
40   FOR R = 1 TO 30
50   READ C(I)
60   LET I = I + 1
70   NEXT R
```

_____

_____

_____

_____

_____

_____

* * * * *

This segment is correct as is but not very efficient.  If we use R as the subscript in line 50, we can take lines 30 and 60 out of the program.  I hope your segment looks like this:

```
20   DIM C(30)
40   FOR R = 1 TO 30
50   READ C(R)
70   NEXT R
```

4- Assume the data in the sample program are arranged so that the 20 ID numbers are in the first DATA statements and the 20 unit prices are included in the next group of DATA statements. Code the BASIC statements that will store these data in lists N and P.

_____

_____

_____

_____

_____

* * * * *

This problem requires two FOR/NEXT loops to do the job, as follows:

```
10   DIM N(20), P(20)
20   FOR J = 1 TO 20
30   READ N(J)
40   NEXT J
50   FOR K = 1 TO 20
60   READ P(K)
70   NEXT K
```

In this segment, you could have used J as the index variable and the subscript in both FOR/NEXT loops. Whenever a FOR/NEXT loop is completed, you may reuse the index variable.

## Back to the Sample Program

Line 240 prints the column headings for the invoice register. Notice that this PRINT statement is not put in a loop. We only want to print the headings once. You could have put this PRINT statement at the beginning of the program at line 40 right after the DIM statement.

Line 250 READs a transaction, including the customer name, the ID number, and the number of units purchased. Line 255 checks for the end-of-data. These are familiar BASIC statements and need no further explanation.

## The Search Routine

Many business applications use tables and lists to store data. These lists are then searched to find the data needed at that time. Some examples are income tax withholding tables, freight rate tables, and parcel post rate tables. These tables are often in human-usable form, but may be included in computer applications.

In the sample program, we have stored product ID numbers and unit prices in two lists. We can now instruct the computer to search through the ID list to find the ID number

in the list that matches or is equal to the ID number from
the transaction, as follows:

```
300   FOR K = 1 TO 20
305   IF I = N(K) THEN 400
310   NEXT K
320   PRINT 'INPUT ERROR FOR'; C$
350   GO TO 250
```

Line 300 starts a loop which will cycle up to 20 times.
The variable K is named as the index variable.  At line 305,
the transaction ID number, I, will be compared to each ID
number in list N.  The index variable, K, is used as the
subscript to identify the specific storage cells in list N.
A specific example will help you to understand this search
process.  List N is as follows:

List N

| 1 | 2 | 3 | 4 | 5 | 6 | 7 | 8 | 9 | 10 |
|---|---|---|---|---|---|---|---|---|----|
| 123 | 128 | 130 | 143 | 150 | 152 | 154 | 158 | 161 | 164 |
| 11 | 12 | 13 | 14 | 15 | 16 | 17 | 18 | 19 | 20 |
| 165 | 167 | 171 | 175 | 177 | 179 | 190 | 195 | 196 | 199 |

When the first transaction data are read at line 250, CPU
storage will look like this:

| C$ | I | U |
|---|---|---|
| Jane Adams | 130 | 100 |

The search routine is started with the index variable K
equal to 1.  At line 305, the value stored in I, 130, is
compared to the value stored in N(1), 123.  Since 130 does not
equal 123, the computer continues to line 310 and then returns
to line 300 where K is set equal to 2.  The value stored in I,
130, is now compared to the value stored in N(2), 128.  These
values are again not equal.  The computer then sets K equal to
3.  The value in I, 130, is now compared to the value stored

in N(3), 130.  The condition in the IF statement at line 305
is TRUE—this is called a <u>hit</u>.  The computer then branches to
line 400 and continues to process the first transaction,
prints the appropriate detail line, and then returns to line
250 to read the next transaction.

When the second transaction data are read at line 250, CPU
storage will be

| C$ | I | U |
|----|---|---|
| Bob Aaron | 167 | 10 |

The search routine is started again, with the index variable
K being reset to 1.  The value stored in I, 167, is compared
to the value stored in N(1), 123, at line 305.  The comparison
is false so the computer continues to line 310 and then
returns to line 300 to loop again with K = 2.  A hit will not
occur until K = 12.  At that time, the computer will branch to
line 400 to calculate the amount and then to print the detail
line for BOB AARON.

The search routine is then repeated for each transaction.
However, sometimes input data are incorrectly entered as at
line 603 in Figure 4-2:  DATA FRED HUBERT, 667, 50.  Notice
that the product ID number, 667, is an incorrect ID number.
In this case, no equal condition will be found in the IF
statement at line 305.  The program will loop through the
search routine 20 times and then branch to the statement
following NEXT K, line 320.  The computer will print the error
message and the customer's name.  After the "run" is finished,
the computer people can find those items that are in error,
make the needed corrections, and reprocess the corrected
transactions.

There are several points you should notice in this search
routine:

1- The search routine should be programmed so that one
   transaction data element is compared to each data
   element in a previously stored list.  The search stops

when you get a hit.  See line 305 in the sample
program.

2-  The index variable in the FOR statement should range
    from 1 to the maximum size of the list as defined in
    the DIM statement.  See lines 30 and 300 in the sample
    program.

3-  The variable that names the list(s) in the DIM state-
    ment must be the same throughout the program.  See
    lines 30, 125, 305, 400, and 410.

4-  The variable used as the subscript in the IF statement
    must be the same as the index variable named in the
    FOR statement.  See line 305.

5-  There should be some way to keep input errors from
    producing output errors.  When no hit can occur, some
    type of error routine should be included in the
    program.  See line 320.

Now It's Your Turn

1-  Correct any errors you find in this exercise.  Assume
data have been stored in list X.

```
10   DIM X(500)
 .    . . .
50   READ Z
60   FOR A = 1 TO 1000
70   IF Z = Y(A) THEN 100
80   NEXT A
100  . . .
```

_____

_____

_____

_____

_____

*****

There are three errors in this program segment.  If you
didn't find all three, try again.

Your corrections should be

```
60   FOR A = 1 TO 500     OR     10   DIM X(1000)
```

The maximum value of the index variable, A, should not be greater than the size of list X as defined the DIM statement.

```
70  IF Z = X(A) THEN 100
```

The name of the list must not be changed in a program.

```
90  PRINT 'INPUT ERROR'
95  GO TO 50
```

If any input errors occur, your program should show that an error is present.

2-  Correct any errors you find in this exercise.  Assume data have been stored in list K.

```
  5   DIM K(100)
  .   . . . .
 20   READ X
 30   FOR J = 1 TO 100
 40   IF X = J(K) THEN 100
 50   NEXT K
 60   PRINT . . .
  .   . . .
100   . . .
```

_____

_____

_____

_____

*****

There are two lines that need correcting.

```
40  IF X = K(J) THEN 100
```

The name of the list was changed and the index variable in the FOR statement was not used as the subscript.

```
50  NEXT J
```

You must be sure that FOR/NEXT statements are paired with the same variable.

3-  Refer to the sample program, Figure 4-2.  Explain what
will happen if lines 320 and 350 are omitted and the incorrect
data at line 603 are read at line 250.

_____

_____

_____

_____

_____

*****

No equal condition will be found at line 305.  The FOR/NEXT
loop will complete its 20 cycles, and the program will then
continue to line 400 with the index variable equal to 21.  The
computer will not be able to find a storage cell named P(21) at
line 400 and will print an error message.  All processing will
then stop.  Some computer systems may handle this error in a
different way.  But, in any case, the computer will stop
processing or incorrect output will occur.

## Making Calculations with Subscripted Variables

When the computer finds an equal condition at line 305, the
program branches to line 400 to calculate the amount due from
that customer.

```
350   . . .
400   LET A = P(K) * U
410   . . .
```

The only new idea in line 400 is P(K).  Remember that list
P contains the price for each product.  Also, the data for
lists N and P were read and stored in pairs so that a product's
ID number and its price were stored in the same storage cells
in the two lists.  For example, the data for the first product
are 123 and 4.50.  N(1) holds 123, and P(1) holds 4.50.  When
we use P(K) in the LET statement, the price stored in that cell

in list P will be paired with the appropriate product ID
number, and the correct amount, A, will be calculated.

Let's reproduce the first five data elements for lists N
and P as they are stored in the CPU:

List N

| 1 | 2 | 3 | 4 | 5 | ... | 20 |
|---|---|---|---|---|-----|----|
| 123 | 128 | 130 | 143 | 150 | ... | 199 |

List P

| 1 | 2 | 3 | 4 | 5 | ... | 20 |
|---|---|---|---|---|-----|----|
| 4.50 | 1.25 | 6.08 | 10.50 | 2.25 | ... | 1.60 |

Remember that the product ID number for the JANE ADAMS
transaction is 130.  When the search routine gets its hit for
this transaction, the index variable K equals 3.  This value
of K is saved, and line 400 works like this:

```
400   LET A = P(K) * U
            = P(3) * U
            = 6.08 * 100
            = 608
```

When the third transaction for BILL QUINCY is processed,
the product ID is 128.  The search routine gets a hit when K
equals 2.  Line 400 then looks like this:

```
400   LET A = P(K) * U
            = P(2) * U
            = 1.25 * 50
            = 62.50
```

You should remember that each time a new transaction is
read the search routine is started over again.  This restart
of the search routine sets the index variable back to 1 so
that each data element of list N is compared to the new
product ID until a hit is made.  When the search is completed,
the value of the index variable is saved and may be used
later in the program.

Now It's Your Turn

1- Assume the following transaction data:

     606  DATA FRED JONES, 199, 30

Show how line 400 in the sample program will work.

     400  LET A = P(K) * U

_____

_____

_____

*****

     Your answer should look like this:

     400  LET A = P(K) * U
                = P(20) * U
                = 1.60 * 30
                = 48

Remember that the search routine will get its hit when K
equals 20—ID number 199 is stored in N(20).  The value of K
is saved and used as the subscript for list P in line 400.

Printing from Subscripted Variables

     Line 410 prints out one detail line for each transaction
after the search routine has found the correct price and the
LET statement has calculated the amount owed us:

     400  . . .
     410  PRINT C$, N(K), U, P(K), A
     450  . . .

This statement will print the customer's name, the product
ID number from list N, the number of units purchased, the
price per unit from list P, and the amount calculated at line
400.  The value of the subscript, K, is still saved from the
search routine.  For the first transaction, K = 3, and line
410 therefore becomes

     410  PRINT C$, N(3), U, P(3), A

The computer prints out the following detail line:

     JANE ADAMS     130          100          6.08          608

For each transaction, the search routine finds the equal condition, the value of the index variable is saved, and the index variable is used as a subscript to select the needed value from the list or lists.

The output from the sample program is shown in Figure 4-3.

| NAME | PRODUCT ID | UNITS | PRICE | AMOUNT |
|------|-----------|-------|-------|--------|
| JANE ADAMS | 130 | 100 | 6.08 | 608 |
| BOB AARON | 167 | 10 | 12.5 | 125 |
| BILL QUINCY | 128 | 50 | 1.25 | 62.5 |
| INPUT ERROR FOR FRED HUBERT | | | | |
| HELEN GONE | 175 | 12 | 2.1 | 25.2 |
| NANCY HOBBS | 152 | 25 | 3.89 | 97.25 |

Figure 4-3

Sample Program—Output for Invoice Register

This PRINT statement is similar to those we discussed before.  You now know that you can print values from one or more lists.  Just be sure to include a subscript.

Let's code a program segment that will print out the ID number and the price lists:

```
 .   . . .
700  FOR L = 1 TO 20
705  PRINT N(L), P(L)
710  NEXT L
 .   . . .
```

Notice that the variable L is used as the index variable in the FOR/NEXT statements and that L is also used as the subscript in the PRINT statement.  This segment will cause the following output to occur:

| | |
|---|---|
| 123 | 4.5 |
| 128 | 1.25 |
| 130 | 6.08 |
| 143 | 10.5 |
| . | . . |
| 199 | 1.6 |

Now It's Your Turn

1- Correct any errors you find in line 410 below.  Assume
that you wish to print the same output as in the sample program
and that this statement is part of that program.

    410  PRINT C$, I, U, P(K), A

_____

\*\*\*\*\*

    Did you make a correction?  None was necessary; this
statement will print the same output as the original line 410.
The value stored in I is equal to the value stored in
N(K)—line 305.

2- Assume that the dollar values of sales for 50 salesmen
have been accumulated in list D.  Each salesman is identified
by a number ranging from 1 to 50.  Code a program segment
that will print out the salesman's number and the accumulated
value of the sales he made.

    10  DIM D(50)
     .  .  .  .

_____
_____
_____
_____
_____

\*\*\*\*\*

    100  FOR K = 1 TO 50
    105  PRINT K, D(K)
    110  NEXT K

Since each salesman is identified by a number from 1 to
50, we can print his ID number using the index variable K.
The value stored in list D is also selected by using K as the
subscript.

Summary of New Concepts in Sample Program

1- Each list to be used in a program must be defined using a DIM statement. The DIM statement names the list with a variable and specifies the maximum number of storage cells in the list. The size specification may be larger than actually needed but must not be smaller.

2- Storing data in lists requires the use of FOR/NEXT statements and a READ statement. The index variable in the FOR statement is used as the subscript in the READ statement.

> BASIC does provide another way for storing data in a list. This will be discussed in Chapter 5.

3- A search routine is used to find an appropriate value in a list. The search usually includes an IF statement within a FOR/NEXT loop. When a hit is made, the program often branches to another part of the program to process the transaction. The saved value of the index variable is used as a subscript to select an appropriate value from one or more lists.

4- Calculations and output can be made using values selected from one or more lists.

NOW IT'S YOUR TURN PROBLEM—SALES AGENT BONUS

Your problem is to accumulate the dollar value of sales made by a firm's 25 sales agents. You are then to find the agent who sold the greatest amount and to compute a 10% bonus for that agent. You should then print out the agent's identification number and the amount of the bonus. The agents' identification numbers range from 1 to 25. The input will consist of data for each sale made and will include the agent's ID number and the dollar value of that sale. Figure 4-4 is a program flowchart giving you a solution to this problem.

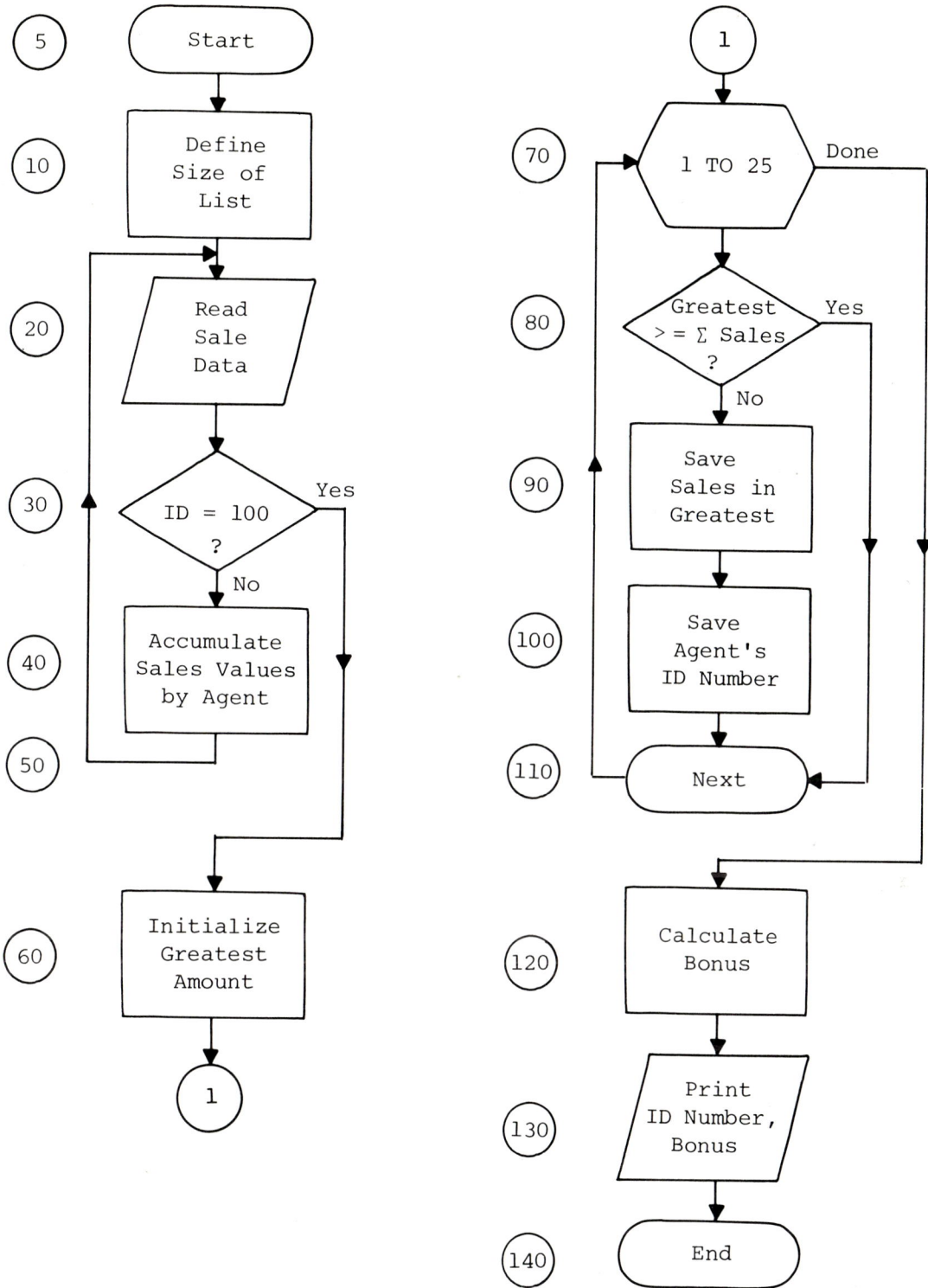

Figure 4-4

Program Flowchart—Sales Agent Bonus

> If you go through your solution in a step-by-step
> way, you will find this problem easy to code.
> Just study the program flowchart and the
> suggestions for completing each line, and if
> you are not sure, return to the chapter and
> review the material.  Do not sneak-a-peak at the
> suggested solution statement until you have really
> tried to figure it out for yourself.

Note:  Assume that your computer sets all storage spaces
equal to zero when your program is stored.

Line 5:  This is an easy one for you to start with.  Identify
the program.

       5 _____

*****

       5   REM SALES AGENT BONUS

Line 10:  This line should define a list in which you will be
able to accumulate the total sales for each of the 25 agents.
Let's use the variable S for "sales."

       10 _____

*****

       10  DIM S(25)

This is the only list we will need in this program.  Since the
agent's ID numbers range from 1 to 25, we will be able to
accumulate the sales values in this list, using the ID number
as the subscript.

Line 20:  Each transaction consists of the agent's ID number
and the dollar value of one sale.  The program flowchart shows
that these data are to be entered in the CPU.

       20 _____

*****

       20  READ I, D

This one should have been easy for you.  I tried to use variable names to give some hint of the data—I for agent's ID and D for dollar value.  You could have used N for number and V for value, but your variable names should not be X and Y. These don't tell you anything.

Line 30:  The flowchart shows a decision to test for last data. We do not have an agent numbered 100.  (Hint!)

    30 _____

*****

    I hope that you started your statement with IF, like this:

    30  IF I = 100 THEN 60

Of course, your line 30 may be different only in respect to the variable name you used to identify the agent.  The THEN 60 came from the TRUE branch in the flowchart.

Line 40:  Watch this one.  You want to accumulate all the dollar values of all sales for a particular agent in list S. For example, you want all sales for agent #5 to be accumulated in S(5), etc.

    40 _____

*****

    The accumulation will work best this way:

    40  LET S(I) = S(I) + D

Remember, the agent's ID number is named I and the dollar value of that sale is named D.  Here is an example:  DATA 5, 450.

    When these data are READ at line 20, CPU storage will look like this:

List S

| I | | D | | . | 3 | 4 | 5 | 6 | 7 | . |
|---|---|---|---|---|---|---|---|---|---|---|
| 5 | | 450 | | . | 0 | 0 | 0 | 0 | 0 | . |

Now, line 40 will work like this:

```
S(I) = S(I) + D
S(5) = S(5) + 450
S(5) = 0    + 450
S(5) = 450
```

The next time a sale is recorded for agent #5, the 450 stored in S(5) will be added to the value of that sale. This same process will work for all 25 agents. Try another example.

How will line 40 work for DATA 22, 325? Assume that agent #22 has already accumulated $600 of sales.

```
S(I) = S(I) + D
```

_____

_____

_____

_____

**\*\*\*\*\***

Your answer should look like this:

```
S(22) = S(22) + D
S(22) = 600 + 325
S(22) = 925
```

<u>Line 50</u>: Another easy one for you. You want to cause the computer to branch back to read the next transaction.

    50 _____
**\*\*\*\*\***

    50  GO TO 20

Need I say more?

Line 60:  At this point in our program, we have read all the transactions and accumulated all the sales amounts for each sales agent.  Lines 60 through 110 search out the greatest amount of accumulated sales, store that amount, and store the ID number of the agent eligible for the bonus.

Line 60 is used to set up a storage area in which to store the greatest value and to initialize that storage area to a value smaller than any possible amount of accumulated sales.

```
    60 _____
*****
```

```
    60  LET G = 0
```

I used the variable G to represent "greatest" and set G equal to zero.  We will discuss how we use this CPU storage area later in the program.

Line 70:  You now want to set up a loop so that each value stored in list S can be compared to G, the greatest value. This should be easy.

```
    70 _____
*****
```

```
    70  FOR K = 1 TO 25
```

This FOR statement will cause the index variable K to equal from 1 to 25.  We can use K as a subscript for list S at line 80.

<u>Line 80</u>:  In this statement, you want to tell the computer to find out whether or not the value stored in G is greater than one value stored in list S.  If G is greater than a value in S, you don't want the computer to do anything except return to the FOR statement so that the next value in S can be tested. Study the flowchart carefully to make sure you get the right line number after THEN.

80 _____

\*\*\*\*\*

If you are using the same variables I am, your answer must look like this:

    80  IF G >= S(K) THEN 110

Notice that I used the index variable K from the FOR statement to step through the values stored in list S.  Also, I told the computer to branch to line 110 if the condition was true.

> In BASIC, you cannot branch from within a FOR/NEXT loop to the FOR statement.  If you want to continue the loop, you must branch to the NEXT statement so that the computer can execute the FOR statement correctly.

<u>Line 90</u>:  The computer will execute line 90 only when the value stored in G is less than a value stored in one cell in list S.  This would mean that the value in list S is greater than the value in G.  Since you want to store the greatest value in G, you should tell the computer to place the greater value from list S in G.

90 _____

\*\*\*\*\*

If you think about this one and study the flowchart carefully, you should have coded the following:

    90  LET G = S(K)

This statement tells the computer to store the value of S(K) in G.  When the computer loops through these IF and LET statements 25 times, the greatest value stored in list S will end up stored in G—just what we want.

Line 100:  When we have finished this part of the program, we want to be able to identify the sales agent who sold the greatest dollar amount.  To do this, we must save the ID number of that agent.

    100 _____
*****

    100  LET N = K

Again, the program will not execute line 100 unless a value stored in list S is greater than the value stored in G.  Each time we store a larger value in G, we must also save the ID number of the agent.  Since the ID number is the same as the value of the index variable K, we can store the value of K in N.

Line 110:  The program flowchart shows you that you are to close the loop.  You should have no trouble with this one.

    110 _____
*****

There is only one answer you can give for this one:

    110  NEXT K

Now, let's look at an example to see how this group of statements works.  Assume that CPU storage looks like this:

| G | | N | | List S | | | | | |
|---|---|---|---|---|---|---|---|---|---|
| | | | | 1 | 2 | 3 | 4 | 5 | . |
| 0 | | 0 | | 350 | 225 | 410 | 375 | 630 | . |

The first time line 80 is executed, K = 1, so the IF statement works like this:

    80  IF G >= S(K) THEN 110
        IF G >= S(1) THEN 110
        IF 0 >= 350  THEN 110

As you can see, the condition is false, so the computer continues to line 90, which does this:

```
90  LET G = S(K)
    LET G = S(1)
    LET G = 350
```

The computer now continues to line 100.  At this point in the program, K = 1.  Line 100 will work this way:

```
100  LET N = K
     LET N = 1
```

CPU storage will now look like this:

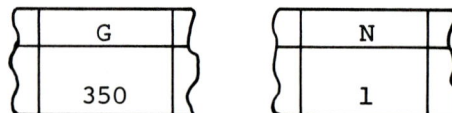

| G |
|---|
| 350 |

| N |
|---|
| 1 |

The values in list S will not be changed.

When the computer continues the loop for the second time, K equals 2.  The IF statement at line 80 now works as follows:

```
80  IF G >= S(K) THEN 110
    IF G >= S(2) THEN 110
I   IF 350 >= 225 THEN 110
```

The condition is true, so the computer then branches to line 110.  There is no change in the values stored in G and N.  The NEXT statement returns the program to the FOR statement where K becomes 3.  The IF statement again compares the value stored in G to a value stored in list S, as follows:

```
80  IF G >= S(K) THEN 110
    IF G >= S(3) THEN 110
    IF 350 >= 410 THEN 110
```

The condition is false, so the computer continues to line 90, sets G = 410 and then at line 100 sets N = 3.

Assume that the value stored in S(5) is the greatest value.  When the FOR/NEXT loop has been completed, the values stored in G and N will be 630 and 5.

<u>Line 120</u>:  After the FOR/NEXT loop is done, we have the
greatest value from list S stored in G and the agent's ID
stored in N.  We are now ready to calculate the bonus.  The
amount of the bonus is equal to 10% of the accumulated sales
for the winning agent.

    120 _____

*****

    This should be another easy statement for you.  I hope
you used B for bonus and that you remembered to convert 10%
to .10.

    120  LET B = G * .10

<u>Line 130</u>:  All you need to do now is to print out the winning
agent's ID number and the amount of his bonus.  Of course,
you should also print some kind of message so that we know
what the numbers are all about.

    130 _____

*****

    Your line 130 should look something like this:

    130  PRINT 'AGENT NUMBER'; N; ' IS THE WINNER.  HIS BONUS IS $'; B

Your message may be different from the one I suggest, but
you should have included the variables N and B in your PRINT
statement.

    You could have omitted line 120 and made the bonus
calculation in the PRINT statement at line 130, like this:

    130  PRINT 'AGENT NUMBER'; N; ' IS THE WINNER.  HIS BONUS IS $'; G * .10

<u>Line 140</u>:  This line tells the computer that the program is
completed.

    140 _____

*****

    140  END

I feel I am insulting your intelligence to include this statement as part of the test.  But it is required at the end of all BASIC programs.

I suggest that you test-run your completed program on your computer, using the following data:

```
5, 100, 17, 325, 11, 250, 1, 400, 4, 250, 3, 220, 7, 143, 24, 450,
5, 300, 8, 150, 20, 315, 6, 412, 4, 750, 9, 80, 3, 225, 25, 500,
19, 150, 4, 300, 17, 180, 11, 410, 100, 0
```

SUMMARY

The primary focus in this chapter has been on one-dimensional arrays or lists.  You should have learned that a list is a group of storage cells in which you store one kind of data.  A specific storage cell in a list is referenced by a subscripted variable, e.g. $X(J)$.  The variable X names the list, while the subscript (J) specifies the numeric position of one cell in the list.

You should also remember that a FOR/NEXT loop is used to READ and store data into a list.  The index variable in the FOR statement is used as the subscript.  You may also accumulate data in a list by using one input data element as a subscript value.  We can also use values from a list in calculations and as output.

Only one new BASIC statement was presented in this chapter:

1-  DIM                 Defines a list by giving it a name
                        (variable) and specifies the maximum
                        number of data elements that may be
                        stored in the list—a numeric
                        constant enclosed in parentheses.

   <u>line number</u>  <u>DIM</u> <u>whole number enclosed in parentheses</u>


EXERCISES

A-  Write a BASIC program segment that will tell the computer to print sales agents' ID numbers and the accumulated values for our firm's 25 sales agents from the "Now It's Your Turn" programming problem in this chapter.

B- Write a BASIC program segment that will find the agent who had the smallest accumulation of sales (same problem as exercise A).

C- Assume you have READ and stored 50 data values in list Z. Write a program segment that will accumulate those values and print the result.

D- Assume the same list Z as in Exercise C. Also, assume that some of the data values are negative. Write a program segment that will print only the positive values, five values per print line.

E- Assume the same list Z as in Exercise D. Write a program segment that will store only the negative values in list Y in the same order as those appearing in list Z. Do not leave any blank cells in list Y.


PROBLEMS

1- We operate a retail store with 20 charge account customers. (We really have 2000, but we want to keep this problem simple!) Each customer has an account number of three digits. Some owe us money (accounts receivable), and others have a zero balance.

Our problem is to process this week's transactions (purchases and payments) with the accounts receivable data and to produce a current accounts receivable report for management.

| | |
|---|---|
| Output | Report title: ACCOUNTS RECEIVABLE--current date |
| | Column headings: CUSTOMER  CURRENT BALANCE |
| | Detail line: Customer number, amount owed |
| | Summary line: TOTAL A/R, total of accounts receivable |
| Input | Customer account number, dollars owed. (There are 20 pairs of these data, so they should be stored in two lists.) |
| | Transaction data: Customer number, transaction type (1 = purchase, 2 = payment), dollar amount of transaction |

| | |
|---|---|
| <u>Process</u> | Store customer number and dollars owed in two lists.<br>Search customer number list for hit.<br>Add purchases to dollar balance.<br>Subtract payments from dollar balance.<br>Accumulate total accounts receivable. |
| <u>Transfer</u> | Transaction type.<br>Last transaction data.<br>Customer number—list equal to customer number—transaction. |
| <u>Test data—20 customers</u> | 345, 25.00, 150, 0, 920, 52.00, 835, 10.50, 532, 0, 461, 2.00, 380, 12.00, 760, 0, 608, 42.75, 185, 15.00, 933, 0, 411, 20.00, 903, 8.00, 222, 1.50, 474, 0, 199, 33.35, 207, 0, 112, 250.00, 565, 0, 106, 2.00 |
| <u>Test data—Transactions</u> | 222, 1, 50.00, 461, 2, 2.00, 345, 1, 50.00, 565, 1, 10.00, 760, 1, 5.50, 815, 2, 20.00, 608, 1, 7.25, 222, 2, 51.50, 760, 1, 10.50, 411, 2, 20.00, 112, 2, 100.00, 806, 2, 50.00, 150, 1, 12.50, 835, 1, 10.50, 0, 0, 0 |

2-  We wish to reward our outstanding sales agents by giving them a 5% bonus.  But we also want to dismiss those sales agents who are not selling enough to pay their salaries.  We have accumulated the dollar value of each of our 25 sales agents' sales for the year.  We will pay the bonus to those agents whose total sales are more than one standard deviation above the mean.  We will dismiss those agents whose total sales are less than two standard deviations below the mean.

| | |
|---|---|
| <u>Output—Report 1</u> | Title:  BONUS REPORT<br>Column headings:  AGENT NUMBER    TOTAL SALES   BONUS<br>Detail line:  Agent's number, total sales, amount of bonus |
| <u>Output—Report 2</u> | Title:  DISMISSAL REPORT<br>Column headings:  AGENT NUMBER    TOTAL SALES<br>Detail line:  Agent's number, total sales |
| <u>Input</u> | Agent number, total annual sales.  (There are 25 pairs of these data.) |
| <u>Process</u> | Store input data in two lists.<br>Compute mean and standard deviation (see Problem 2, page 123).<br>Search total sale list for values greater than |

mean plus 1 x standard deviation, calculate
bonus, print Report 1.
Search total sale list for values less than mean
minus 2 x standard deviation, print Report 2.

Transfer                Total sale > mean plus 1 x standard deviation.
                        Total sale < mean minus 2 x standard deviation.

Test data               41, 5600, 32, 9750, 79, 12500, 64, 10250, 49,
                        15800, 86, 9860, 71, 21250, 90, 19830, 31,
                        8440, 67, 18500, 25, 22900, 33, 18100, 44,
                        17900, 55, 15600, 28, 24300, 45, 19900, 66,
                        10980, 77, 16500, 88, 20150, 99, 20333, 98,
                        13550, 87, 19825, 76, 21980, 54, 17750, 43,
                        18760

3-  Rewrite Problem 1 in Chapter 2, using a list to store the
pay rates.  The output, processes, and test data are the same
as those in Chapter 2.  You will have to read and store the
five pay rates in a list and use the wage class to select the
appropriate pay rate for each employee.

# 5

# Two-Dimensional Arrays—Tables

INTRODUCTION

In Chapter 4, you were introduced to the idea of lists or one-dimensional arrays.  You even worked through some programs using lists.  Many business applications can be handled with one or more lists.  But in some statistics and management science applications, it is much easier to use tables.

When you have mastered this chapter, you will

1- Know about tables, including the concept of row and column subscripts.

2- Store data in a table and print values from a table.

3- Use a table to accumulate data values within certain classifications.

4- Enter data into a table or list using a MAT statement.

5- Output values from a table or list using a MAT statement.

6- Use MAT statements to manipulate values in tables or lists.

PROGRAMMING CONCEPTS

A table is rectangular and contains rows and columns of storage cells.  As with lists, a table has only one name, a variable.  Each storage cell within the table is referred to

by <u>two</u> subscripts, a row subscript and a column subscript.
A table called Q with three rows and four columns will look
like this:

Table Q

| 1,1 | 1,2 | 1,3 | 1,4 | Row 1 |
|-----|-----|-----|-----|-------|
| 2,1 | 2,2 | 2,3 | 2,4 | Row 2 |
| 3,1 | 3,2 | 3,3 | 3,4 | Row 3 |

Col. 1      Col. 2      Col. 3      Col. 4

There are 12 storage cells in table Q. Each cell is
identified by two numbers, the first number referring to the
row position and the second number referring to the column
position. For example, Q(1,4) refers to the cell in row 1,
column 4—in the upper right-hand corner of table Q.

If we want to store 25.67 in row 2, column 3 of Q, we
should write

    51   LET Q(2,3) = 25.67

Or we could write the following statements and store 25.67 in
the same cell in Q:

```
35   LET I = 2              35   LET I = 2
40   LET J = 3        OR    51   LET Q(I,I + 1) = 25.67
51   LET Q(I,J) = 25.67
```

As you can see, table subscripts may be numbers, variables,
or expressions, just as with a list.

Storing Data in a Table

To store data in a table, we will use FOR/NEXT statements
just as we did when working with lists. We will use nested
loops and the index variables as the row and column subscripts.

The program segment shown below will store 12 data values in table Q:

```
12   DATA 3, 5, 7, 2, 4, 9, 1, 5, 7, 8, 10, 3
20   FOR J = 1 TO 3
25   FOR K = 1 TO 4
30   READ Q(J,K)
35   NEXT K
40   NEXT J
50   . . .
```

After this program segment has been executed, table Q will look like this:

Table Q

| 1,1 | 1,2 | 1,3 | 1,4 |
|-----|-----|-----|-----|
| 3   | 5   | 7   | 2   |
| 2,1 | 2,2 | 2,3 | 2,4 |
| 4   | 9   | 1   | 5   |
| 3,1 | 3,2 | 3,3 | 3,4 |
| 7   | 8   | 10  | 3   |

In this example, J is the row subscript and K is the column subscript.  From our discussion of nested FOR/NEXT loops in Chapter 3, you should remember that the inner loop goes through its complete cycle for each value of the outer loop.  Therefore, when J = 1, K will equal 1, then 2, then 3, and then 4.  So when the READ Q(J,K) is executed the first time, J equals 1 and K equals 1.  The first data element, 3, will be stored in Q(1,1).

The second time the READ is executed, J will still equal 1, but K will equal 2.  The second data element, 5, will be stored in Q(1,2)—the first row and second column.

> When the column subscript is controlled by the inner loop, the DATA values are stored in the table by rows.  The four columns of first row are filled, then the four columns of the second row, then the four columns of the third row.

If we make the row subscript the inner loop, then the
data will be stored by columns, and the three rows of the
first column will be filled first, then the rows in the second
column, etc.  The following program segment will store the
same data in table R by columns:

```
12   DATA 3, 5, 7, 2, 4, 9, 1, 5, 7, 8, 10, 3
20   FOR K = 1 TO 4
25   FOR J = 1 TO 3
30   READ R(J,K)
35   NEXT J
40   NEXT K
```

Now, R will look like this:

Table R

| 1,1 | 1,2 | 1,3 | 1,4 |
|-----|-----|-----|-----|
| 3   | 2   | 1   | 8   |
| 2,1 | 2,2 | 2,3 | 2,4 |
| 5   | 4   | 5   | 10  |
| 3,1 | 3,2 | 3,3 | 3,4 |
| 7   | 9   | 7   | 3   |

Notice that the data are stored in different cells in the
two arrays.  The contents of the first row in table Q is 3, 5,
7, 2, but the first row of table R is 3, 2, 1, 8.

In most business applications using two-dimensional arrays,
the storage cells in which data are stored are extremely
important.  Therefore, you should study the problem carefully
and make sure you enter the data in the proper cells.

## Using Data Stored in a Table

We can tell the computer to do many different things to
data that are already stored in a table.  We can total the
values stored in each column or the values stored in each row.
We can find the arithmetic mean (average) of all the values,
or we can find the largest or the smallest value stored in
that table.  In each of these examples, we must use nested

FOR/NEXT loops so that the row and column positions of the table can be specified.

Let's assume that we want to search through table R to find all values greater than 5 and to print out each of those values.

The following program segment will do this for us:

```
 .   . . .
 60  FOR N = 1 TO 4
 70  FOR M = 1 TO 3
 80  IF R(M,N) <= 5 THEN 100
 90  PRINT R(M,N)
100  NEXT M
110  NEXT N
 .   . . .
```

Notice that the index variable N is the column subscript and that M is the row subscript.  Each time we refer to table R, M must be the first subscript.  The comparison at line 80 will be made 12 times.  When the value stored in a cell is less than or equal to 5, the program skips the PRINT statement.  But when the value is greater than 5, the IF condition at line 70 is false and the computer continues to line 90 to print the value.

The first time the IF statement is executed, both N and M will equal 1.  The value in R(1,1) is 3, which is less than 5.  The computer branches to line 100, returns to line 70 where M is set equal to 2.  The value in R(2,1) is 5 which is equal to 5.  The computer again skips to line 100, returns to line 70, and M is set equal to 3.  The value stored in R(3,1) equals 7.  The condition is false, so the computer continues to line 90 and prints 7, the value stored in R(3,1).

The inner loop is now done, so the computer continues to line 110.  The NEXT N returns control to line 60, where N is set equal to 2.  The M loop now starts over at 1.  Twelve comparisons will be made, and the output will be 7, 9, 7, 8, and 10.

We could have written this program segment so
that it fits more closely the problem statement—
"PRINT all values greater than 5."

```
 .    . . .
 60   FOR N = 1 TO 4
 70   FOR M = 1 TO 3
 80   IF R(M,N) > 5 THEN 90
 85   GO TO 100
 90   PRINT R(M,N)
100   NEXT M
110   NEXT N
 .    . . .
```

Notice the comparison at line 80 has been reversed.
But notice also the added statement at line 85.

## Printing Values from a Table

After you have created a table in the CPU, you often want
to print the data in the same form.  Since most printing
devices print horizontally across the page, you should be
careful to cause the output to be by rows.  You print all the
columns in row 1, then all the columns in row 2, etc.  For
example, the following program segment will print the values
from table R:

```
 .    . . .
200   FOR Y = 1 TO 3
210   FOR Z = 1 TO 4
220   PRINT R(Y,Z),
230   NEXT Z
240   PRINT
250   NEXT Y
 .    . . .
```

This segment will cause the values stored in R(1,1),
R(1,2), R(1,3), and R(1,4) to be printed on the first line.
The values stored in row 2, R(2,1), R(2,2) etc., will be
printed on the second line, and the row 3 values will be
printed on the third line.

> Remember, the dangling comma (at the end of
> line 220) causes the computer to print each value
> on one line.  If we had not used the dangling
> comma, all 12 values of table R would have been
> printed on 12 lines in the first print zone.

The "empty" PRINT statement at line 240 causes a "blank"
to be printed at the end of each row.  Since there is no
dangling comma, the printer automatically spaces to the next
line after this PRINT statement.

Now It's Your Turn

1- Correct any errors you find in the following program
segment.  Assume you want to store data elements in table B
with four rows and two columns.

```
20   FOR J = 1 TO 8
30   READ B(J,K)
40   NEXT K
45   DATA . . .
```

_____

_____

_____

_____

_____

*****

There is very little that is correct in this program
segment, but here is one way to make it correct.

```
20   FOR J = 1 TO 4
25   FOR K = 1 TO 2
30   READ B(J,K)
40   NEXT K
41   NEXT J
45   DATA . . .
```

Whenever we work with a two-dimensional array or table, we
must use two subscripts—therefore the two FOR/NEXT loops.
Also, we must be sure that the index variables are the same
in any one FOR/NEXT loop.

2-  Assume you wish to store the eight data elements in array

B (Exercise 1) by columns.  You want to store the first four
data elements in column 1 and the last four in column 2.
Write a program segment to do this.

_____

_____

_____

_____

_____

*****

Your answer should look like this:

```
20  FOR K = 1 TO 2
25  FOR J = 1 TO 4
30  READ B(J,K)
35  NEXT J
40  NEXT K
45  DATA . . .
```

The program in Exercise 1 stored data by rows—the first
row is filled, then the second, etc.  So the only change you
needed to make was to reverse the order of the FOR/NEXT loops.

> When you want to READ or PRINT a table by rows,
> you make the FOR/NEXT loop that controls the
> row subscript the outer loop.  When you want to
> READ or PRINT by columns, you make the column
> FOR/NEXT loop the outer loop.

3- Assume that 20 data values have been stored in table V
with five rows and four columns.  Code the statements that
will cause the computer to print that table.  Print the first
row, then the second row, and so forth.

_____

_____

_____

_____

_____

*****

The only real problem with this exercise is deciding

whether the row subscript should be the inner or outer loop.
This is what your answer should look like:

```
 50   FOR N = 1 TO 5
 60   FOR M = 1 TO 4
 70   PRINT V(N,M),
 80   NEXT M
 90   PRINT
100   NEXT N
  .   . . .
```

I certainly hope you didn't cross your loops.  Notice
that the N loop controls the rows and is the outer loop.
Also, notice the comma after the PRINT statement at line 70.
This will cause four column values to be printed on one
line.  If you left the comma out, the computer will print all
20 data values in one column in the first print zone.  The
"empty" PRINT statement at line 90 is required so that the
computer will space to the next print line after the four
columns are printed on each line.


SAMPLE PROBLEM

Our problem is to analyze the sales of five different
products in three different sales districts.  We want to
accumulate the value of each product sold in each district.

1- Study the problem.  The major output will be a table
   showing the sales for each product in five rows and
   the sales in each district in three columns.  The
   total sales for product #2 made in district #2 will
   show in the table in the second row, second column.
   The input will be one data set for each sale and will
   include the product number (1, 2, 3, 4, or 5), the district
   number (1, 2, or 3), and the dollar value of that sale.
   The processes will be to accumulate the individual
   sales amounts in the appropriate row (product) and
   the appropriate column (district) in the table.
   There will have to be a last data decision, but the
   product-district decisions can be made automatically.
   This will be shown and discussed in the explanation
   of the program.

2-   Plan the solution.  Figure 5-1 is a program flowchart
     showing one way to solve this problem.
3-   Code the computer program.  Figure 5-2 is a
     translation of the planned solution in the Figure 5-1
     flowchart into BASIC.

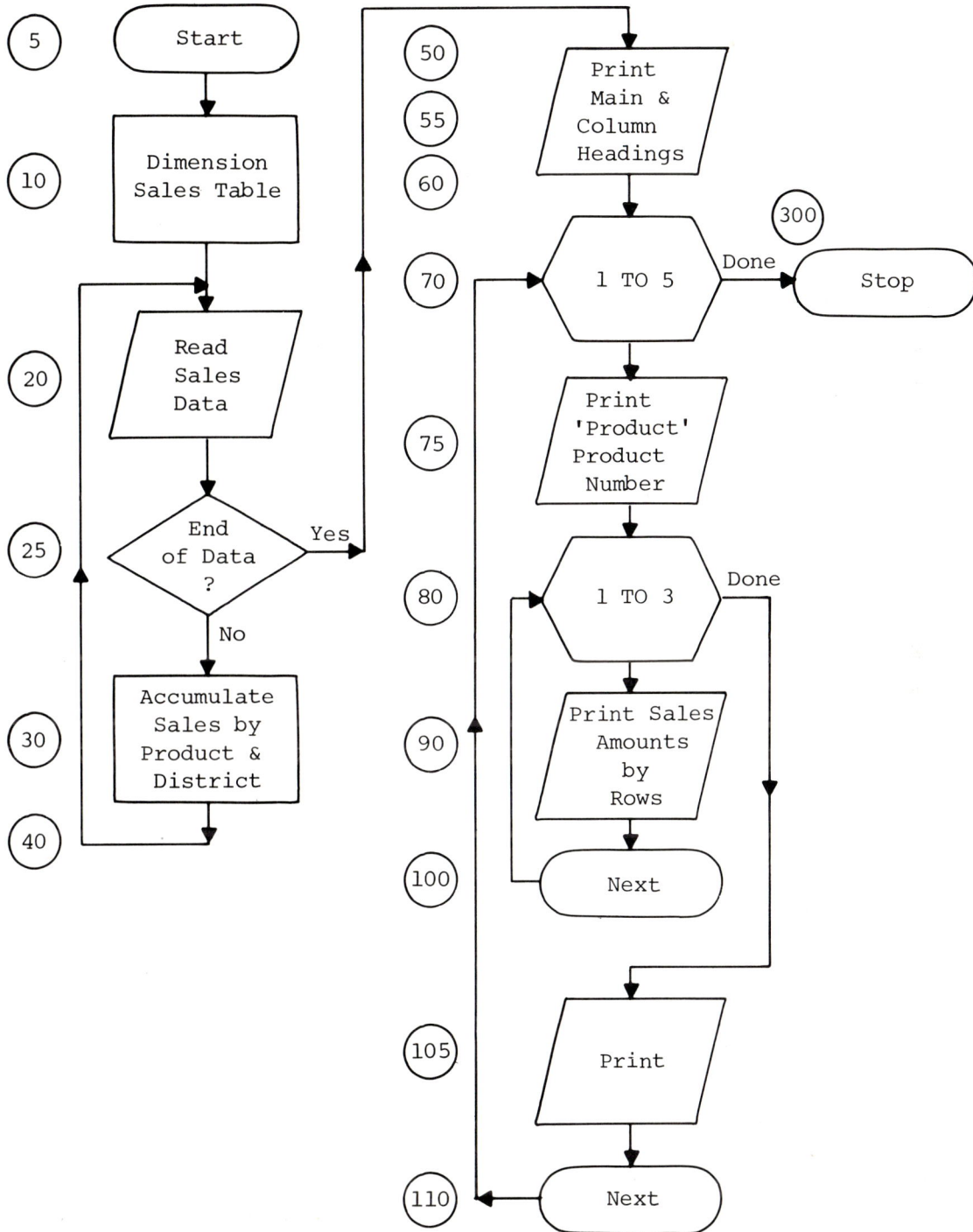

Figure 5-1

Program Flowchart—Sales Analysis

```
  5   REMARK SALES ANALYSIS
 10   DIM S(5,3)
 20   READ P, D, A
 25   IF P = 0 THEN 50
 30   LET S(P,D) = S(P,D) + A
 40   GO TO 20
 50   PRINT TAB (25), "SALES ANALYSIS"
 55   PRINT
 60   PRINT TAB (13); "DISTRICT 1"; TAB (28); "DISTRICT 2";
 61   PRINT TAB (43); "DISTRICT 3"
 65   PRINT
 70   FOR N = 1 TO 5
 75   PRINT "PRODUCT"; N,
 80   FOR M = 1 TO 3
 90   PRINT S(N,M),
100   NEXT M
105   PRINT
110   NEXT N
200   DATA 4,1,150,2,3,200,3,1,400,5,2,180,1,3,200,2,2,250,1,3,450
210   DATA 5,1,75,3,2,175,4,2,100,3,3,600,4,1,280,1,1,300,2,1,125
220   DATA 5,3,75,1,2,120,3,3,200,1,2,80,2,1,75,4,3,120,5,1,125
230   DATA 0,0,0
300   END
```

Figure 5-2

BASIC Program—Sales Analysis

EXPLANATION OF BASIC STATEMENTS

This program uses many programming statements and
techniques with which you are familiar.  You already know
about the END OF DATA decision at line 25 and the PRINT (TAB)
statements at lines 50, 60, and 61.  However, you will need
some help with line 30 where we accumulate the sales amounts
in table S.  Also, causing the table to print correctly is
tricky.

Defining Two-Dimensional Arrays

```
  5   . . .
 10   DIM S(5,3)
 20   . . .
```

This statement names the table S and specifies that it
will contain five rows and three columns.  The table is named
with a simple variable which should hint at the data the
table is to hold.  In this program, I named the table "S" to
indicate "sales."  The numbers within the parentheses specify

the size of the table; the first specifies the number of
rows, and the second specifies the number of columns.  These
must be whole numbers, not variables or decimal numbers.

You may dimension more than one list or table with one
DIM statement, as follows:

    5  DIM A(25,4), C(10), X(2,10)

In this DIM statement, table A is specified with 25 rows and
4 columns, a total of 100 storage cells.  List C contains 10
storage cells, and table X has 2 rows and 10 columns.

---

Most computer systems do not require that you
dimension lists of 10 or fewer storage positions
or tables with 10 or fewer rows and 10 or fewer
columns.  In the DIM statement above, list C and
table X would not have to be dimensioned.  The
computer system will automatically dimension any
list with 10 storage positions and any table with
10 rows and 10 columns or 100 storage positions.

However, much storage space is wasted if you do
not dimension your tables.  For instance, table S
in the sales analysis program would automatically
be set with 10 rows and 10 columns—100 storage
positions rather than just 15 when the DIM
statement is used.  Also, when we use the MAT
statements, each table or list must be dimensioned.
We will discuss MAT statements later in this
chapter.

---

The general form of the DIM statement is

| | | |
|---|---|---|
| 1- | Line number | Must precede each BASIC statement. |
| 2- | DIM | Key word telling computer to set aside storage positions for one or more lists or tables. |
| 3- | Array name | A simple variable used to identify the list and/or table. |
| 4- | Array size | Two numbers, separated by a comma, enclosed in parentheses.  The first whole number specifies the maximum number of rows in the table, and the second specifies the maximum number of columns.  Most computer systems will automatically dimension a list with ten rows and a table with ten rows and ten columns. |

Now It's Your Turn

1-  Write the BASIC statement(s) that will define a table
containing 20 rows and 5 columns.

_____

*****

     10  DIM T(20,5)

The only difference between your DIM statement and that
shown above is the table name and the line number.  Remember
that the row subscript must be first.

2-  Correct the errors, if any, in the following BASIC
statement:

     5   LET N = 25
     6   LET M = 40
     10  DIM Z(N,M)

_____

_____

_____

*****

     10  DIM Z(25,40)

Remember that the values within the parentheses must be whole
numbers—they may not be variables even when those variables
have been previously defined.

3-  Write the statement(s) that will define one-dimensional
array(s) to hold the customer numbers, accounts receivable
balances, and date of last payment for 1000 charge account
customers.

_____

*****

     5   DIM N(1000), B(1000), D(1000)

You may have used different names for these three lists, but
other than that, your answer should be just like mine.

4-  Now write the statement(s) that will define a two-
dimensional array to store the customer data described above.

_____

*****

Your DIM statement should look like this:

5  DIM C(1000,3)

In this table, the 3 data elements about each customer will
be stored in the 1000 rows.  The 3 columns will store the
customer number, accounts receivable balance, and date of
last payment, in that order.

### Back to the Sample Program

The READ statement at line 20 causes the three data
elements for each sale to be stored in the CPU.  Remember
that the data for each sale include the product number, the
district number, and the amount of the sale.  As you will see,
we will use the product and district numbers to accumulate
the sales amounts according to the desired product and district
numbers.

The IF statement at line 25 is used to check for the end
of the data and causes the computer to end the loop in which
we accumulate the sales amounts in table S.

### Accumulating Values in a Table

```
25  . . .
30  LET S(P,D) = S(P,D) + A
40  . . .
```

Line 30 is the most important statement in the sample
program.  This LET statement is an "adding machine" which
accumulates the sales amounts in table S according to the
product and district numbers.  To see how this will work, let's
assume that the first three data elements at line 200 have
been READ.  CPU storage will look like this:

| P | | D | | A |
|---|---|---|---|---|
| 4 | | 1 | | 150 |

When we refer to S(P,D) in line 30, we specify storage position S(4,1). Remember, we read in a value for P and for D. Line 30 therefore adds the amount stored in S(4,1) to the amount stored in A and stores the sum in S(4,1). Before line 30 is executed, S(4,1) will contain

Table S

| 4,1 |
|-----|
| 0 |

Line 30 will work this way:

```
30   LET S(P,D) = S(P,D) + A
         S(4,1) = S(4,1) + A
         S(4,1) = 0 + 150
         S(4,1) = 150
```

So, after line 30 is executed, S(4,1) will hold

Table S

| 4,1 |
|-----|
| 150 |

The next time the data elements specify product 4 and district 1 (the fifth set of data in line 210), CPU storage will look like this:

Table S

| P | D | A | 4,1 |
|---|---|---|-----|
| 4 | 1 | 280 | 150 |

And line 30 will work this way:

```
30   LET S(P,D) = S(P,D) + A
         S(4,1) = S(4,1) + A
         S(4,1) = 150     + 280
         S(4,1) = 430
```

Now, CPU storage for product 4, district 1 in table S will be

Table S

| 4,1 |
|-----|
| 430 |

After all the data have been processed, when $P = 0$, the first row in table S will look like this:

Table S

| 1,1 | 1,2 | 1,3 |
|-----|-----|-----|
| 300 | 200 | 650 |

Now It's Your Turn

1-  In the space below, draw table S showing the row and column subscripts.  I suggest you use table Q at the beginning of this chapter as a model.

*****

Your table S should look like this:

Table S

| 1,1 | 1,2 | 1,3 |
|-----|-----|-----|
| 2,1 | 2,2 | 2,3 |
| 3,1 | 3,2 | 3,3 |
| 4,1 | 4,2 | 4,3 |
| 5,1 | 5,2 | 5,3 |

> Notice that the first subscript is the same
> in each row (across).  In the first row, the
> first subscript is 1, and in the last row,
> the first subscript is 5.  Also, you can see
> that the second subscript is the same for
> each column (down).  In the first column, the
> second subscript is 1, and in the last column,
> the second subscript is 3.

2-  Using the data from lines 200, 210, and 220, accumulate
the sales amounts in table S above.  Think like a computer,
and follow the directions given at lines 20 and 30 in the
sample program.
*****

    After all the data have been processed, table S should
look like this:

Table S

| 1,1 | 1,2 | 1,3 |
|-----|-----|-----|
| 300 | 200 | 650 |
| 2,1 | 2,2 | 2,3 |
| 200 | 250 | 200 |
| 3,1 | 3,2 | 3,3 |
| 400 | 175 | 800 |
| 4,1 | 4,2 | 4,3 |
| 430 | 100 | 120 |
| 5,1 | 5,2 | 5,3 |
| 200 | 180 | 75  |

    You should have read the first three data elements at
line 200:  4, 1, and 150.  You then should have found row 4
and column 1 in table S and added the sales amount, 150, to
the amount then stored in that cell.  Then you should have
read the next set of data elements at line 200 (2, 3, and 200),
found row 2 and column 3, and added the sales amount, 200,

to the value then stored in that cell.  You should have
repeated these steps until you read the end-of-data elements
at line 230.  If the values you placed in table S were not
the same as those shown above, I suggest that you try this one
again.

## Back to the Sample Program

Lines 50 through 65 print the report heading and the
column headings.  Please notice that these lines are not
included within the loop that accumulated the sales amounts
in table S, nor within the loops that print out the completed
table.

```
 40   . . .
 50   PRINT TAB (25); "SALES ANALYSIS"
 55   PRINT
 60   PRINT TAB (13); "DISTRICT 1"; TAB(28); "DISTRICT 2";
 61   PRINT TAB(43); "DISTRICT 3"
 65   PRINT
 70   . . .
```

Line 50 causes the printer to indent 25 spaces before printing
the report title.  Line 55 outputs a blank line, and lines
60 and 61 space the three column headings in the second, third,
and fourth print zones.  And you know what line 65 is supposed
to do.

## Printing the Values from Table S

The next segment of the sample program, lines 70 through
110, will print out the body of the table as well as the
word PRODUCT and the product number.  The values of the
table should be printed out one row at a time.

```
  65   . . .
  70   FOR N = 1 TO 5
  75   PRINT "PRODUCT"; N,
  80   FOR M = 1 TO 3
  90   PRINT S(N,M),
 100   NEXT M
 105   PRINT
 110   NEXT N
 200   . . .
```

Line 70 in this program segment establishes the outside

loop, and the index variable N will become the row subscript.
When N is equal to 1, the computer will be printing the values
from the first row of table S, and when N equals 2, the
second row, etc.

Line 75 will cause the computer to print, in the first
print zone, the word PRODUCT, and immediately following the
current value of N, the product number.  Remember that the
semicolon makes the print zone smaller.  Also, the trailing
or dangling comma at the end of line 75 will keep the
computer from spacing and will therefore allow the printer to
print the remaining values on one print line.

Line 80 controls the inner loop and establishes M as the
column subscript.  Since table S contains three columns, the
values of M may be 1, 2, and 3.  When M equals 1, the values
from the first column of table S will be printed.  Also, when
M equals 2, the values from the second column will be printed,
etc.

Line 90 will cause the computer to print the values from
table S one row at a time.  When N is equal to 1 and M is
equal to 1, the value stored at S(1,1) will be printed.  The
computer will then continue to line 100, the NEXT M statement,
which will cause the computer to return to line 80 and set M
equal to 2.  The PRINT statement at line 90 will then print
the value from S(1,2).  The dangling comma at the end of
line 90 will cause the second column value to be printed on
the same line.

While N is equal to 1, the computer will print the word
PRODUCT, the product number, and the three values stored in
the first row of table S.  The output will look like this:

```
PRODUCT 1       300         200             650
```

After this line is printed, the inner loop is done.  The PRINT
statement at line 105 causes a blank to print in the fifth
print zone, and since there is no dangling comma, the printer
spaces to the next print line.

The NEXT statement at line 110 returns the program to

line 70 where N is set to 2.  The second line of the report
is printed as follows:

PRODUCT 2          200              250              200

Lines 70 through 110 are repeated five times under the control
of the FOR statement at line 70.  When that loop is done,
the entire report has been printed, and the program is
completed by the END statement at line 300.  Figure 5-3 shows
how the completed report will look.

SALES ANALYSIS

|            | DISTRICT 1 | DISTRICT 2 | DISTRICT 3 |
|------------|------------|------------|------------|
| PRODUCT 1  | 300        | 200        | 650        |
| PRODUCT 2  | 200        | 250        | 200        |
| PRODUCT 3  | 400        | 175        | 800        |
| PRODUCT 4  | 430        | 100        | 120        |
| PRODUCT 5  | 200        | 180        | 75         |

Figure 5-3

Printed Output—Sample Problem

Now It's Your Turn

1-  Assume the sample program had been coded like this:

```
 70  FOR N = 1 TO 5
 75  PRINT "PRODUCT N"
 80  FOR M = 1 TO 3
 90  PRINT S(N,M)
100  NEXT M
105  NEXT N
```

Show the printed output that will occur when N = 1.

_____

_____

_____

_____

_____

*****

Your output should look like this:

```
PRODUCT N
300
200
650
```

You should remember that any characters enclosed in quotes in
a PRINT statement will be printed just as shown within the
quotes.  Therefore, the letter N is printed, not the value
stored in N.  Also, the lack of the dangling commas at the
end of lines 75 and 90 allows the printer to space to a new
print line after each print statement is executed.  If this
program segment were run, as is, the output would all appear
in the first print zone on 20 print lines.

2-  Assume the sample program had been coded like this:

```
 70   FOR N = 1 TO 5
 75   PRINT "PRODUCT"; N,
 80   FOR M = 1 TO 3
 90   PRINT S(N,M),
100   NEXT M
110   NEXT N
```

Show the printed output for N = 1, then N = 2, and then N = 3:

———————————————————————————————————————————————————

———————————————————————————————————————————————————

———————————————————————————————————————————————————

———————————————————————————————————————————————————

*****

Here is what you should have printed:

```
PRODUCT 1      300      200      650        PRODUCT 2
200            250      200      PRODUCT 3   400
175            800
```

Messy, isn't it?  Leaving out the "empty" PRINT statement at
line 105 lets the printer use all five print zones.  Remember,
the output is supposed to appear in four columns, not five.

Summary of Key Ideas in the Sample Problem

There are several key ideas that were presented in the sample problem, as follows:

1- A two-dimensional array or table must be defined with two subscripts in the DIM statement. Each time you refer to a table within the program, you must use two subscripts.

2- It is not necessary for you to read and store data into the table. Data can be accumulated or calculated into a table. In the sample program, the data were accumulated by using a product number and a sales district number as the two subscripts so that the values could be accumulated in the appropriate row and column according to the product number and district number, respectively.

3- We were able to print out the report with appropriate headings. We were careful to label the columns and to name the product rows. By using the dangling commas and the "empty" PRINT statement, we were able to control the printed output so that our report was easily read.

NOW IT'S YOUR TURN PROBLEM—EXTENDED SALES ANALYSIS

Your problem will be to continue the report produced in the sample problem. The sales manager wants to know the total sales for each product and the total sales for each district. First, you will have to add up the sales for each product (compute the total for each row in table S). Second, you will have to add up the sales for each district (compute the total for each column in table S).

You should also print out the column headings PRODUCT and

TOTAL SALES for the first part of this report and the headings
DISTRICT and TOTAL SALES for the second part.  Your report
should include one line for each product, showing the product
number and the total sales.  The same type of information
should be included in the district sales report.  Figure 5-4
is a partial flowchart to help you code this part of the
sales analysis program.

Please notice that we have continued the flowchart from
Figure 5-1.  Rather than ending the program at line 300, we
will continue with the next segment after the original report
is completed.  Your job is to write the BASIC statements that
will solve this problem.  Follow the flowchart and the
suggestions given for each line(s).

Lines 300, 301, 302, 303:  These lines should put two blank
lines between the two parts of our SALES ANALYSIS report,
print the required column headings, and print one blank line
after the headings.

```
300 _____
301 _____
302 _____
303 _____
```
*****

```
300  PRINT
301  PRINT
302  PRINT "PRODUCT", "TOTAL SALES"
303  PRINT
```

The "empty" PRINT statements at lines 300 and 301 cause the
printer to leave two blank lines.  The column headings will
be placed in the first two print zones, and then 303 leaves
one blank line.

Line 305:  In this part of the problem, you want to accumulate
the sales amounts in each row.  This statement should start
the loop to control the rows.

```
305 _____
```
*****

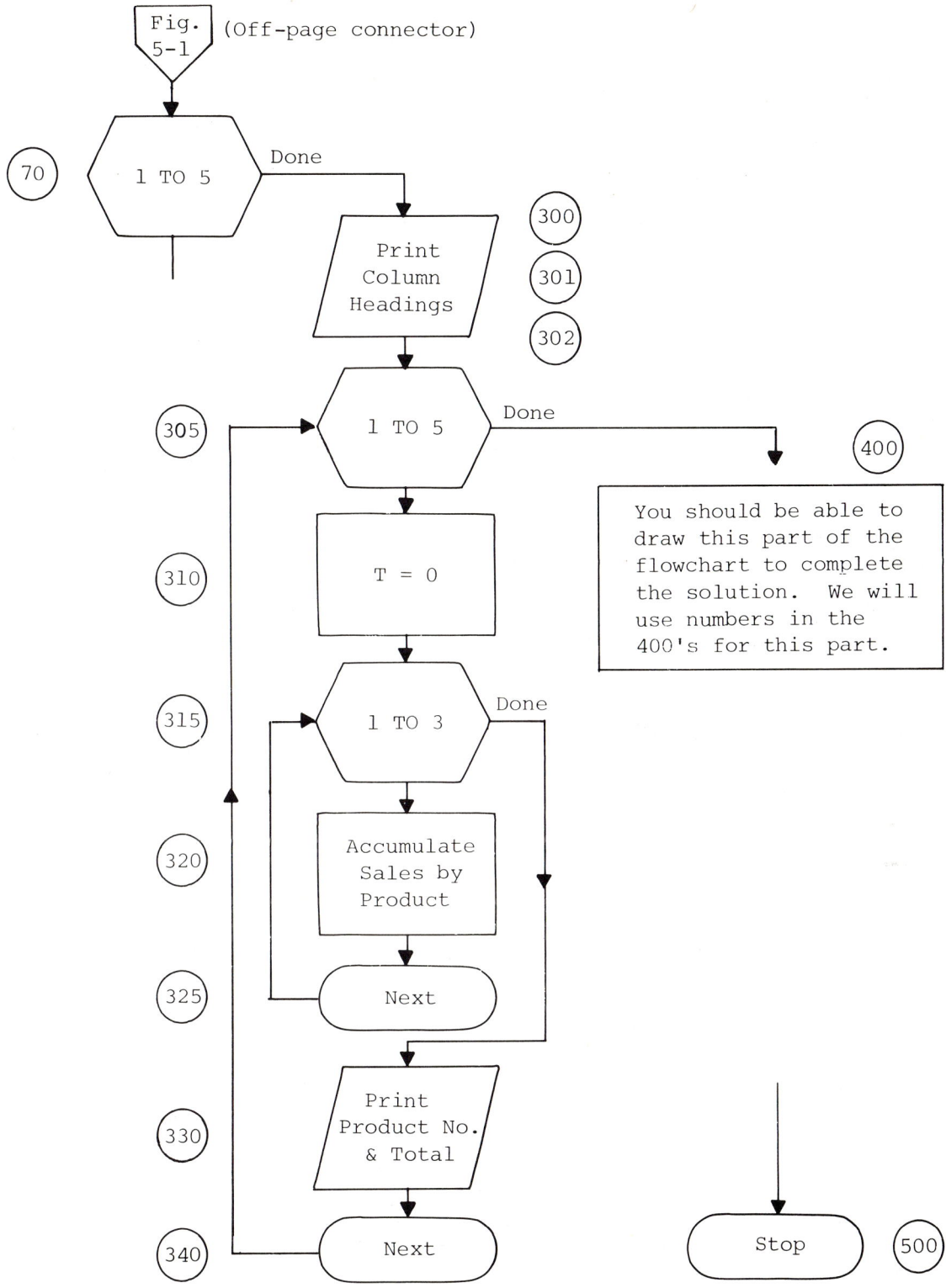

Figure 5-4

Program Flowchart—Extended Sales Analysis

I would code this line like so:

    305  FOR N = 1 TO 5

Remember that there are five rows in table S; therefore you must tell the computer to loop five times.

Line 310:  You need to accumulate the total for each row. You need to "clear" your "adding machine" before you start, so you need to set that storage area equal to zero.

    310 _____
*****

    Your statement should be something like this:

    310  LET T = 0

I used T because it reminds me of TOTAL.  You could have used any variable if it were not used for something else in the program.  This statement will be executed each time you start adding up values in a new row.

Line 315:  You want to add up the amount stored in each column in each row of table S.  This statement should start a loop to control the columns.

    315 _____
*****

    315  FOR M = 1 TO 3

Line 320:  Here you want to add up the three values in each row of table S and save those values in your "adding machine," T.

    320 _____
*****

    Watch this one!

    320  LET T = T + S(N,M)

The first time this statement is executed, N and M both equal 1.  The value stored in S(1,1) is added to T, and the result is stored in T.  During the second execution, N equals 1, but M equals 2.  The value stored in S(1,2) is added to T, and the result is stored in T.  This happens one more time with M equal to 3.  The "adding machine," T, now contains the total found in the three columns of the first row of table S.

Line 325:  You need to close the inner loop so that it can go around the required three times.  This is an easy one.

    325 _____

*****

Just make sure you use the right index variable, the one you used at line 315:

    325  NEXT M

Line 330:  This line should print the body of this report segment, including the product number and the total sales for that product.

    330 _____

*****

This statement should be easy if you remember that the FOR statement at line 305 controls the rows and that N will therefore represent the product number.

    330  PRINT N, T

Line 340:  We are now through with the total for Product 1. We need to return to start processing the total for Product 2.

    340 _____

*****

This one should look like this:

    340  NEXT N

When the computer is done with this part of the program, lines 300-340, the total sales for each product will have been printed.  In the next section, you should print the appropriate column headings, accumulate the sales by columns, and print

out the total for each column.  You will notice in Figure 5-4
that I have not completed the flowchart.  You should do that
before you try to code each BASIC statement.  Use the same
line numbers but make them 400's rather than 300's.

Lines 400, 401, 402, 403:  These lines should print a couple
of blank lines, the appropriate column headings, and another
blank line.

```
400 _____
401 _____
402 _____
403 _____
```
*****

I am sure your BASIC statements look like this:

```
400  PRINT
401  PRINT
402  PRINT "DISTRICT", "TOTAL SALES"
403  PRINT
```

Line 405:  Remember, in this part of the program, you want
to add up all the values in each column.  You want to add up
the five values in column 1, then those values in column 2,
and then those in column 3.  Is that enough of a hint?

```
405 _____
```
*****

You should have coded a FOR statement to loop for the
columns like this:

```
405  FOR J = 1 TO 3
```

Line 410:  You need to clear your "adding machine."

```
410 _____
```
*****

This is a simple statement.  Yours should look something
like this:

```
410  LET T = 0
```

<u>Line 415</u>:  You should add up the amounts stored in each row
for each column.  This statement should start a loop to do
this.

415 _____

*****

How many are there?  Your FOR statement should look like
this:

415  FOR K = 1 TO 5

<u>Line 420</u>:  This one should be very similar to line 320.  You
want to accumulate the values in each column and store the
result in your "adding machine."

420 _____

*****

You must be careful that your subscripts for table S are
in the right order.

420  LET T = T + S(K,J)

Since J controls the columns and K controls the rows, you
must be sure that K is the first subscript within the
parentheses.  When this statement is first executed, both J
and K equal 1.  Therefore, the value stored in S(1,1) is
added to T, and the result is stored in T.  The second time
line 420 is executed, K equals 2, and J still equals 1.  The
value stored in S(2,1) is added to T.  This is repeated five
times.  The values stored in each of the five rows in column
1 of table S are accumulated in T.

<u>Lines 425 through 440</u>:  No more hints or suggestions.  You try
to complete this program on the basis of your flowchart segment.

425 _____
430 _____
440 _____
500 _____

*****

Assuming that we are continuing the sample program in
Figure 5-2, this program segment should look like this:

```
300  PRINT
301  PRINT
302  PRINT "PRODUCT", "TOTAL SALES"
303  PRINT
305  FOR N = 1 TO 5
310  LET T = 0
315  FOR M = 1 TO 3
320  LET T = T + S(N,M)
325  NEXT M
330  PRINT N, T
340  NEXT N
400  PRINT
401  PRINT
402  PRINT "DISTRICT", "TOTAL SALES"
403  PRINT
405  FOR J = 1 TO 3
410  LET T = 0
415  FOR K = 1 TO 5
420  LET T = T + S(K,J)
425  NEXT K
430  PRINT J, T
440  NEXT J
500  END
```

If you had trouble with this exercise, I suggest you return to
the first part of the chapter and review the "using data" and
"printing values" sections.  Also, you could refer to Figure
5-4 and work your way through lines 305-340.  Use some scratch
paper to keep track of the values of N, M, and T.  Then repeat
the process for lines 405-440.  In the space below, show what
the printed output would look like after this program segment
is run.

*****

Your answer should look like this:

| PRODUCT | TOTAL SALES |
|---------|-------------|
| 1 | 1150 |
| 2 | 650 |
| 3 | 1375 |
| 4 | 650 |
| 5 | 455 |

| DISTRICT | TOTAL SALES |
|----------|-------------|
| 1 | 1530 |
| 2 | 905 |
| 3 | 1845 |

MANIPULATION OF TABLE VALUES

In many management science and statistics problems, you will use two or more tables or lists. BASIC appears to be easier to use for the manipulation of matrices (tables) than other programming languages. One common situation is to add the values stored in two tables and store the result in a third table.

Addition of Tables

Suppose that we want to add the elements of two 3 x 4 tables (three rows, four columns) and then print out the table holding the result of our addition. There are three steps required for the solution of this problem:

1- Read the proper values into the two tables.
2- Add the corresponding elements of the two tables and store the sums in a third table.
3- Print out the answer table.

Using Nested FOR/NEXT Loops: Remember that we store data in a table by using nested FOR/NEXT loops. We discussed this at the beginning of this chapter. A program segment that will

store 12 data elements into table A using nested FOR/NEXT
loops will look like this:

```
20  DIM A(3,4)
25  DATA 2, 5, 6, 9, 1, 4, 5, 3, 8, 6, 5, 2
30  FOR I = 1 TO 3
35  FOR J = 1 TO 4
50  READ A(I,J)
60  NEXT J
70  NEXT I
    .  .  .  .
```

This program segment defines table A, gives 12 data
elements, and then reads these elements into table A by rows.

To solve this problem of adding two tables together, we
would need to code a similar program segment to store 12 data
elements in table B.  A third program segment would be needed
to add the elements of table A to those in table B and to
store the results in table C.  Then we would need a fourth
program segment to print out the values of table C.

Using BASIC MAT Statements:  BASIC provides a much simpler
method for manipulating table values than that discussed above.
The program flowchart in Figure 5-5 and the BASIC program in
Figure 5-6 illustrate this simple method.


EXPLANATION OF BASIC STATEMENTS

You are familiar with the REM, DIM, and DATA statements,
I hope.  But the MAT statements are new and will be discussed
below.

MAT READ Statement

```
 5  .  .  .
10  .  .  .
20  MAT READ A, B
30  .  .  .
```

Line 20 causes the computer to read and store 12 data
values into table A and then to read and store the next 12 data
values into table B.  The data are stored row by row.  The
12 data elements in the DATA statement at line 45 are stored

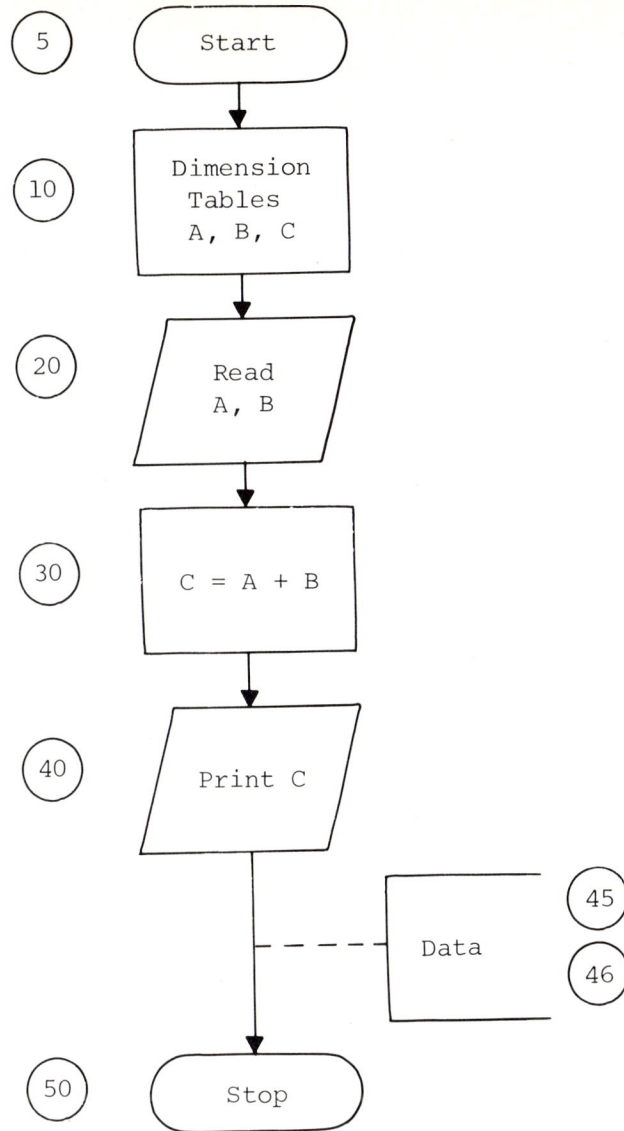

Figure 5-5

Program Flowchart—Add Two Tables, Print Answer Table

```
 5   REM THIS PROGRAM ADDS TWO TABLES, PRINTS ANSWER TABLE
10   DIM A(3,4), B(3,4) C(3,4)
20   MAT READ A, B
30   MAT C = A + B
40   MAT PRINT C
45   DATA 2, 5, 6, 9, 1, 4, 5, 3, 8, 6, 5, 2
46   DATA 3, 6, 9, 1, 2, 7, 9, 4, 3, 7, 2, 9
50   END
```

Figure 5-6

BASIC Program—Add Two Tables, Print Answer Table

in table A, and the data from line 46 are stored in table B.
The first row of table A will look like this after the MAT
READ statement is executed.

Table A

| 1,1 | 1,2 | 1,3 | 1,4 |
|-----|-----|-----|-----|
| 2   | 5   | 6   | 9   |

> In many problems using tables, it is essential
> that you store the data elements in a special
> order.  You should therefore use extreme care
> when entering the values in the DATA statement
> when the MAT READ statement is used.

## Adding Table Values

```
20   . . .
30   MAT C = A + B
40   . . .
```

Line 30 causes the computer to add each element stored in
table A to its corresponding element stored in table B and to
store the resulting sum in the same row-column position in
table C, as follows:

```
C(1,1) = A(1,1) + B(1,1)
C(1,2) = A(1,2) + B(1,2)
C(1,3) = A(1,3) + B(1,3)
  .  .     . . . .
C(3,4) = A(3,4) + B(3,4)
```

If we did not have the MAT statement, the following
program segment would be needed to do this addition:

```
25   FOR L = 1 TO 3
26   FOR M = 1 TO 4
30   LET C(L,M) = A(L,M) + B(L,M)
31   NEXT M
32   NEXT L
```

You can see that the MAT C = A + B statement makes the
addition much simpler.

## Printing a Table

```
30   . . .
40   MAT PRINT C
45   . . .
```

Line 40 will cause the computer to print the values stored in table C.  The DIM statement specified that table C should contain three rows and four columns.  The MAT PRINT statement outputs the values stored in table C in three rows and four columns.

> The output is usually printed in the normal zones with a blank line between each printed line.  On some systems, you may override the normal zone spacing by using a semicolon as with a "regular" PRINT statement.

## BASIC MAT Statements

This sample program has introduced you to three MAT statements.  All BASIC MAT statements are shown below along with a brief description of their function:

| | |
|---|---|
| MAT READ A, B | READs data into lists or tables A and B. |
| MAT PRINT C | PRINTs data from table C. |
| MAT C = A + B | Adds the values in tables A and B and stores sums in table C. |
| MAT C = A - B | Subtracts the values in table B from those in table A and stores differences in table C. |
| MAT X = e * A | Multiplies each data element in table A by the expression e and stores products in table X. |
| MAT Z = X * Y | Multiplies table X by table Y and stores result in Z.  Follows algebraic rules for matrix multiplication. |
| MAT B = TRN(A) | Stores the transpose of table A in table B. |
| MAT K = INV(A) | Calculates the inverse of table A and stores it in table K. |
| MAT L = ZER | Sets each element of table L to zero. |
| MAT M = CON | Sets each element of table M to one. |
| MAT N = IDN | Sets up an identity table N. |
| MAT P = A | Sets table P equal to table A. |

If you are not familiar with matrix algebra and you wish
to use matrices in the solution to any problem, it is suggested
that you study an algebra or management science text before
attempting to apply any of the MAT statements shown above.

## MAT Statements and Lists

Lists also may be manipulated using the MAT instruction.
For example, the BASIC program shown below will read data into
list A; multiply those elements by the expression 3.1417,
storing the products in list X; and print list X.

```
100   DIM A(10), X(10)
110   MAT READ A
120   MAT X = 3.1417 * A
130   MAT PRINT X
150   DATA 3, 4, 9, 1, 5, 7, 2, 8, 3, 7
200   END
```

The general form of the MAT statement used for input or
output is

| | | |
|---|---|---|
| 1- | Line number | Must precede each BASIC statement. |
| 2- | MAT | Key word indicating a list or table. |
| 3- | READ or PRINT | Key word indicating the input of data into a list or table or the output of data from a list or table. |
| 4- | Variable | The name given the list or table. Usually defined in a DIM statement. |

The general form of the MAT statement used for matrix algebra
is

| | | |
|---|---|---|
| 1- | Line number | Must precede each BASIC statement. |
| 2- | MAT | Key word indicating a matrix process. |

3-  Variable              The name given the matrix which
                          will be used to store the results
                          of the manipulation.

4-  =                     Separates variable on its left
                          from matrix expression on its
                          right.

5-  Matrix expression     May be addition, subtraction,
                          multiplication, etc.  Defines the
                          operation to be performed on the
                          matrix or matrices named to the
                          right of equal sign.


SUMMARY

In this chapter, you should have learned about two-
dimensional arrays or tables.  You now know that tables are
rectangular and contain rows and columns in which data may be
stored.  A table is named with a simple variable followed by
two subscripts enclosed in parentheses.  The first subscript
always refers to the row position in the table, while the
second subscript refers to the column position.

You will usually use nested FOR/NEXT statements to enter
data into a table or to print data from a table.  The index
variables from the nested FOR/NEXT statements are usually
used as the subscripts to refer to the rows and columns
within the table.

The MAT instructions were introduced to give you an
easier, more efficient way for processing arrays.  These were
the only "new" statements presented in this chapter.  For a
review of the MAT statements, please refer to pages 194
through 199.

EXERCISES

A-  Code a program segment, using the MAT instruction, that
will store the data in table Q as shown on page 166.  Include
the DATA statement.

B-  Code a program segment, using the MAT instruction, that
will store the data in table R on page 167.  Include the
DATA statement.

C-  Write the BASIC statement(s) that will store 20 odd
integers into table A (5 x 4).  The integers should start with
1.  Do not use a DATA statement.  Store the values so the
first row looks like this:

    1   3   5   7   9

D-  Write the BASIC statement(s) that will place the odd
integers from table A (Exercise C) into list D in ascending
order.

E-  Make any needed corrections in the following program
segments.  Do not make unneeded corrections.

```
1-   30   DIM Z(3,4)
     32   FOR J = 1 TO 4
     34   FOR K = 1 TO 3
     36   PRINT Z(J,K)
     38   NEXT J
     40   NEXT K

2-   40   DIM F(2,3), G(3,2), S(3,3)
     42   FOR I = 1 TO 3
     44   FOR J = 1 TO 2
     46   MAT READ F(J,I), G(I,J)
     48   NEXT J
     50   NEXT I

3-   50   DIM L(2,3), M(3,2), P(3,3)
      .    .   .   .
     60   MAT P = L - M
```

PROBLEMS

1-  Code a BASIC program to accomplish the following:

    a-  Read the following 16 data values into a 4 x 4 matrix
        by rows:
        4, 7, 2, 1, 6, 8, 5, 3, 9, 8, 1, 3, 4, 6, 5, 7.

    b-  Add the values in each column and print the four sums
        with appropriate messages.

    c-  Add the values in each row and print the four sums
        with appropriate messages.

    d-  Add the values in the (1,1) to (4,4) diagonal and print
        the sum with an appropriate message.

    e-  Add the values in the (4,1) to (1,4) diagonal and print
        the sum with an appropriate message.

  Note:  FOR/NEXT loop(s) must be used in parts b, c, d,
and e.

2-  Code a BASIC program to accomplish the following:

    a-  Read the 16 data values shown above into a 4 x 4
        matrix, by columns (i.e., column 1 should contain
        4, 7, 2, 1).  Print this matrix.

    b-  Square each value and store that value into a
        16-position one-dimensional array.

    c-  Print the resulting one-dimensional array with an
        appropriate heading.

    d-  Store the values in the one-dimensional array into a
        4 x 4 array by rows.

    e-  Take the square root of each value.

    f-  Transpose the resulting 4 x 4 matrix and print it with
        an appropriate heading.  This matrix should be
        identical to the original matrix.

3-  Professor Jones wishes to compute the course grades for
his 20 students based on a normal curve.  Each student has
received five grades during the semester, each grade of equal
weight.

Each student's grade will be determined by the relationship
among his total points, the standard deviation of all total
points, and the mean of all total points, as follows:

Total points > 1.5 standard deviations above mean = A

Total points > .5 and <= 1.5 standard deviations above mean = B

Total points ± .5 standard deviation from mean = C

Total points < .5 and >= 1.5 standard deviations below mean = D

Total points < 1.5 standard deviations below mean = F

Print the heading GRADE REPORT and each student's number and
appropriate letter grade.  The data are as follows:

| Student Number | Grade 1 | Grade 2 | Grade 3 | Grade 4 | Grade 5 |
| --- | --- | --- | --- | --- | --- |
| 100 | 23 | 69 | 50 | 19 | 86 |
| 111 | 22 | 65 | 49 | 20 | 93 |
| 122 | 24 | 72 | 38 | 19 | 83 |
| 133 | 20 | 68 | 45 | 17 | 79 |
| 144 | 19 | 56 | 32 | 12 | 58 |
| 155 | 24 | 75 | 40 | 20 | 95 |
| 166 | 15 | 45 | 40 | 15 | 76 |
| 177 | 12 | 35 | 36 | 11 | 49 |
| 188 | 19 | 72 | 28 | 19 | 98 |
| 199 | 22 | 68 | 34 | 16 | 89 |
| 200 | 24 | 54 | 45 | 16 | 98 |
| 211 | 16 | 55 | 39 | 19 | 87 |
| 222 | 19 | 67 | 48 | 20 | 91 |
| 233 | 13 | 56 | 33 | 12 | 66 |
| 244 | 16 | 55 | 31 | 15 | 70 |
| 255 | 9 | 45 | 20 | 11 | 48 |
| 266 | 20 | 74 | 48 | 19 | 99 |
| 277 | 18 | 68 | 41 | 17 | 85 |
| 288 | 16 | 59 | 39 | 19 | 89 |
| 299 | 11 | 41 | 41 | 12 | 79 |

4-  Rewrite Problem 1 in Chapter 4 using a <u>table</u> for the
customer accounts receivable data rather than the two lists.

# 6

# Other BASIC Features

INTRODUCTION

You have now learned enough BASIC programming so that you may
solve almost any business problem.  However, BASIC does give
you some additional features that will increase your
programming effectiveness.  The purpose of this chapter is to
present these features.  When you have completed this chapter
you will know how to use

1- Standard functions.
2- Programmer-defined functions.
3- Subroutines.
4- RESTORE.
5- Files.

STANDARD FUNCTIONS

BASIC gives you ten different mathematical functions that
make your programming easier.  Each of these functions is a
set of instructions written to solve a specialized mathematical
operation.  They are built into BASIC, and you may use any of
them by writing the name of the function.  These functions
are called standard, library, or built-in functions and are
summarized in Figure 6-1.  You will find that some of them are
of little use in typical business problems, while others are
extremely valuable.

You should notice that several of these functions are used
to solve trigonometry problems:  ATN, COS, SIN, and TAN.

Others are primarily mathematical:  ABS, EXP, and LOG.  However,
three of them can be most useful in statistics and management
science applications:  INT, RND, and SQR.  We will pay
particular attention to these last three, but these standard
functions are all used in a similar manner.

| Function | Description |
|----------|-------------|
| ABS(X) | Absolute value of X |
| ATN(X) | Arctangent of X, X in radians |
| COS(X) | Cosine of X, X in radians |
| EXP(X) | Exponent, e, raised to power of X |
| INT(X) | Integer part of X |
| LOG(X) | Natural logarithm of absolute value of X |
| RND(0) | Random number generator; gives a six-digit pseudorandom number between 0 and 1 |
| SIN(X) | Sine of X, X in radians |
| SQR(X) | Square root of absolute value of X |
| TAN(X) | Tangent of X, X in radians |

Figure 6-1

Standard BASIC Functions

When you wish to use one of these standard functions, you
write its three-letter name and enclose a variable, constant,
or expression within parentheses (replace the X).  For
example, assume you want to print the integer part of the
expression A / C.  You would write the following BASIC
statement:

```
200  PRINT  INT(A / C)
```

If A = 15.7 and C = 4, the computer will calculate the answer
to the expression within the parentheses:  (A / C) = 3.925.
The INT function will tell the computer to save and print only
the integer part of that answer, 3.

Here is an example of the SQR function.  In Problem 2 in
Chapter 3, you calculated a standard deviation like this:

```
60  LET X = ((X2 - X1 ** 2 / N)/(N - 1)) ** .5
```

You used the exponent ** .5 to calculate the square root.
You could have used the SQR function like this:

    60  LET S = SQR((X2 - X1 ** 2 / N)/(N - 1))

In these statements X2 = $\Sigma$ X$^2$ and X1 = $\Sigma$ X.  The computer
calculates the answer to the expressions enclosed in the
parentheses and then takes the square root using the SQR
function.


SAMPLE PROBLEM USING FUNCTIONS

In this problem, we wish to simulate 1000 tosses of a
pair of dice.  We want to find out the probabilities of
rolling the different possible outcomes:  2, 3, 4, 5, 6, 7,
8, 9, 10, 11, and 12.  We will need to simulate the roll of
each die (one of the pair), add the two rolls together, and
then keep track of how many times each possible outcome
occurred.  After the 1000 rolls, we will want to print out the
11 probabilities.  The BASIC program shown in Figure 6-2 will
do this simulation for us.

```
 10  REM DICE SIMULATION
 20  DIM D(12)
 30  FOR J = 1 TO 1000
 40  LET R1 = INT(RND(0) * 6 + 1)
 41  LET R2 = INT(RND(0) * 6 + 1)
 50  LET R = R1 + R2
 60  LET D(R) = D(R) + 1
 70  NEXT J
 80  FOR K = 2 TO 12
 90  PRINT "THE PROBABILITY OF ROLLING A"; K; "IS"; D(K) / 1000
100  NEXT K
120  END
```

Figure 6-2

Dice Simulation—Using Functions


Explanation of BASIC Statements

Lines 40, 41, and 60 should be the only statements that
need to be explained.  If you do not understand the other

statements, you should review the appropriate discussion in
Chapters 1 through 5.

```
40   LET R1 = INT(RND(0) * 6 + 1)
```

The possible outcomes for the roll of one die are 1, 2,
3, 4, 5, and 6.  Line 40 simulates the roll of one of the two
dice and stores 1, 2, 3, 4, 5, or 6 in R1.  The RND(0) will
"call" the random number function, which will generate a
decimal number consisting of six digits between .000001 and
.999999 inclusive.  When we multiply this number by 6 and add
1 to that answer, the results will be between 1.000006 and
6.999994.  Then by using the INT function, we tell the computer
to save only the whole-number part of the answer and to store
that value in R1.

```
41   LET R2 = INT(RND(O) * 6 + 1)
```

Line 41 simulates the role of the second die and stores
one of the possible outcomes in R2.

I suggest that you pick some numbers between 0 and 1
[you be RND(0)] and check out this arithmetic.

> Some systems may use values other than zero
> following the function RND, and some do not
> require any value following RND.  Since most
> systems appear to generate the best distribution
> of random numbers when using the zero, I suggest
> that you use zero as your argument in RND.

```
60   LET D(R) = D(R) + 1
```

One of the requirements of this problem is the counting
of the number of times each possible outcome of the roll of
the dice occurs.  Line 60 keeps this tally for us in list D.
For example, if R1 = 2 and R2 = 4, R will equal 6.  The value
stored in list D(6) will be increased by 1.  When all 1000
outcomes have been tallied, list D will hold the number of
times each possible outcome occurred.

The output should look something like this:

```
THE PROBABILITY OF ROLLING A 2 IS .028
THE PROBABILITY OF ROLLING A 3 IS .055
THE PROBABILITY OF ROLLING A 4 IS .083
THE PROBABILITY OF ROLLING A 5 IS .111
THE PROBABILITY OF ROLLING A 6 IS .139
THE PROBABILITY OF ROLLING A 7 IS .167
THE PROBABILITY OF ROLLING A 8 IS .139
THE PROBABILITY OF ROLLING A 9 IS .111
THE PROBABILITY OF ROLLING A 10 IS .083
THE PROBABILITY OF ROLLING A 11 IS .055
THE PROBABILITY OF ROLLING A 12 IS .028
```

Another common use of the RND function is in Monte Carlo simulation techniques. For example, assume we wish to simulate an inventory system. We have found that demand for a particular item in our inventory has the following distribution:

| Demand—Units Per Day | Probability | Cumulative Probability |
|:---:|:---:|:---:|
| 10 | .20 | .20 |
| 11 | .45 | .65 |
| 12 | .30 | .95 |
| 13 | .05 | 1.00 |

The following BASIC program segment will generate a random number, compare the random number to the cumulative probabilities, and set the demand, D, equal to the appropriate value:

```
  .
 50   LET R = RND(0)
 60   IF R <= .20 THEN 100
 65   IF R <= .65 THEN 110
 70   IF R <= .95 THEN 120
 80   LET D = 13
 85   GO TO 150
100   LET D = 10
105   GO TO 150
110   LET D = 11
115   GO TO 150
120   LET D = 12
150   . . .
```

For example, if R = .563419 after line 50, the condition at line 60 will be false. But at line 65, the condition will

be true.  The program will then branch to line 110 where D
will be set equal to 11.  The program then skips to line 150
to continue the inventory simulation.

You should notice that the standard functions used in the
above examples have all been part of an expression.  That is,
each standard function has been on the right-hand side of an
equal sign or part of a "calculating" PRINT statement.  The
following statements using standard functions are not correct:

```
25   READ SQR(X), INT(M), SIN(R)
26   LET INT(A) = X * Y / Z
```

Also, a standard function may be included in an expression
that is being calculated by another standard function.  Lines
40 and 41 in the sample problem illustrate this point.

The general form of standard function is

1-  Function name        Three-letter name provided by
                         manufacturer.

2-  Expression           May be a constant, variable, or
                         arithmetic expression; must be
                         enclosed in parentheses.

```
Most computer systems provide more than 10
standard functions.  For instance, the IBM
5100 system offers 25, and the PDP-11
provides 13.  I suggest you check the
programming manual for the standard functions
available on your computer.
```

PROGRAMMER-DEFINED FUNCTIONS

BASIC also gives you the option of constructing your own
mathematical functions.  One typical business application is
to round dollar and cent values.  In a payroll, for example,
we would like to print paycheck amounts with only two decimal
positions (cents) rounded correctly.  If an employee works
38.3 hours at $4.25 per hour, his gross pay will be computed
equal to 162.775.  We would not want to print his paycheck
with that amount but would want to round this to 162.78.

The BASIC program in Figure 6-3 will prepare a simplified payroll register with all pay amounts rounded correctly.

```
 10   REM PAYROLL REGISTER
 20   DEF FNR(X) = INT(X * 100 + .5) / 100
 25   READ N, H, R
 30   DATA 111, 38.3, 4.25, 222, 41.2, 4.25, 333, 39.1, 4.21, 0, 0, 0
 35   IF N = 0 THEN 150
 40   IF H > 40 THEN 60
 45   LET G = H * R
 50   GO TO 70
 60   LET G = R * 40 + (H - 40) * R * 1.5
 70   LET P = FNR(G)
 80   PRINT N, G, P
 90   GO TO 25
150   END
```

Figure 6-3

Payroll Register—Rounded Pay Amounts

Explanation of BASIC Statements

    20   DEF FNR(X) = INT(X * 100 + .5) / 100

Line 20 is an example of a programmer-defined function. Whenever FNR(A) is used in the program, the mathematical expression to the right of the equal sign (in line 20) is solved using the value stored in A.  At line 70 above, FNR(G) "calls" the function at line 20.  The value of G, from line 45 or 60, is used in the place of X.  The employee's gross pay is rounded to the nearest cent and is stored in P.

The DEF tells the computer that a mathematical function is to be defined—DEF stands for defined.  FNR is the name of the function and is used at line 70 to "call" the function, just as INT was used in the dice simulation problem to "call" the integer function.  Each programmer-defined function name must begin with FN.  The programmer completes the 3-letter name with one of the 26 letters of the alphabet.  In other words, you may include up to 26 defined functions in one program.

The variable X in parentheses is a "dummy" argument and is used in the expression.  When the function is "called," as in line 70, the actual argument, G, is used in the FNR.

The value of G is then used in the expression wherever the dummy variable X appears.  In this example, employee #111 worked less than 40 hours.  His gross pay, 162.775, is calculated at line 45 and stored in G.  Function FNR is "called" at line 70.  The value of G is substituted for X in the expression as follows:  INT(162.775 * 100 + .5) / 100. The rounded answer from this calculation, 162.78, is stored in P.

The output from this program includes the gross pay for each employee, G, as well as the rounded amount of that pay, P.  You will therefore be able to see the effect of the FNR function.

```
111     162.775     162.78
222     177.65      177.65
333     164.611     164.61
```

The general form of the DEF statement is

| | | |
|---|---|---|
| 1- | Line number | Must precede all BASIC statements. |
| 2- | DEF | Key word signaling programmer-defined mathematical function. |
| 3- | FN letter | Names the function; the letter is supplied by the programmer.  Used to "call" the function within the program. |
| 4- | (Variable) | A dummy argument enclosed in parentheses; used in the function expression. |
| 5- | = | Separates function name from expression. |
| 6- | Expression | Mathematical function; may be any valid BASIC arithmetic expression including standard functions and other defined functions. |

This form of the DEF statement may consist of only one line and provides only one numeric value as its answer.  A few systems allow the programmer to define a function with several lines of BASIC statements.  This feature is helpful, but the same result may be achieved using a subroutine which is available on all systems.

---

Some computer systems allow more than one variable in the DEF statement.  These systems include the IBM 5100, IBM 370, PDP-11, General Automation, Honeywell, and Xerox systems.  The following DEF statement is correct for these systems:

    10  DEF FNX(A, B, C) = (A + B+ C) / 3

However, it should be pointed out that any DEF statement may calculate only one value.

---

SUBROUTINES

Some business applications require that the same group of programming instructions be used several times in one program. BASIC gives us a way to write these instructions only once and then to use them anytime we want within a program.  The group of instructions is called a subroutine.

An often-used computation in business statistics is the calculation of factorials.  For example, many problems require the computation of the number of combinations of n things taken r at a time.  The formula for the number of combinations, C, is

$$C = \frac{n!}{r!(n-r)!}$$

(n! is called n factorial.  When n = 5, n! = 5 x 4 x 3 x 2 x 1 = 120.)  If we write a program to calculate C, we will need to computer three different factorials:  n!, r!, and (n - r)!. Rather than repeating the statements needed to calculate these factorials, we can write a subroutine and then use that subroutine three times, as shown in Figure 6-4.

```
10    REM CALCULATE COMBINATIONS
20    PRINT "TYPE VALUES FOR N AND R";
25    INPUT N, R
30    LET F = N
40    GOSUB 100
45    LET N1 = X
50    LET F = R
60    GOSUB 100
65    LET R1 = X
70    LET F = N - R
75    GOSUB 100
80    LET P = X
85    PRINT "THE NUMBER OF COMBINATIONS OF"; N; "THINGS"
86    PRINT "TAKEN"; R; "AT A TIME IS"; N1 / (R1 * P)
90    STOP
100   REM SUBROUTINE TO CALCULATE FACTORIALS
105   LET X = 1
110   FOR A = F to 2 STEP -1
120   LET X = X * A
130   NEXT A
140   RETURN
150   END
```

Figure 6-4

Calculating a Combination with a Subroutine


Explanation of BASIC Statements

In the sample grogram, lines 10 through 90 are the main
program, while lines 100 through 140 are the subroutine.  You
should notice that the subroutine is "called" three times in
the main program:  at line 40, at line 60, and at line 75.

```
40  GOSUB 100
```

The GOSUB statement is used to "call" the subroutine.  When
this statement is executed, the computer branches directly to
the line number given in the GOSUB statement.  This is an
unconditional transfer similar to a GO TO.

For example, when line 40 is executed, the computer jumps
directly to line 100 and continues executing the program from
that point until a RETURN statement is encountered.

```
140  RETURN
```

The RETURN statement tells the computer to leave the subroutine and to return to the main program. When the RETURN statement is encountered, the program jumps back into the main program at the statement immediately following the last executed GOSUB. In the sample program, the RETURN at line 140 causes the computer to jump back to line 45 in the main program.

Again, at line 60, the GOSUB sends the computer to the subroutine at line 100. The RETURN tells the computer to return to line 65. Then at line 75, the subroutine is called again. The RETURN at 140 sends the computer back to line 80.

There are some other statements that make this program work. Remember that we want to calculate the factorials for N, R, and N - R. Also, we want to use only one set of instructions, the subroutine, to make each of these calculations. We wrote the program to accomplish this by including lines 30, 50, and 70. Notice that we assigned the value of N to F at line 30 and that F is used at line 110 in the subroutine to start the factorial loop. We then assigned the value of R to F at line 50 and then called the subroutine. And again at line 70, we gave F the value of N - R. This is called <u>passing</u> values from the main program to the subroutine.

In this program, we must also return values from the subroutine to the main program. We do this at lines 45, 65, and 80. Each factorial is calculated and stored in X at line 120 in the subroutine. At line 45 in the main program, the factorial of N is saved in N1. And at line 65, the factorial of R is saved in R1, while at line 80, the factorial of N - R is saved in P. These three factorials are then used in line 86 to calculate the number of combinations.

```
90  STOP
```

The STOP statement at line 90 is used to keep the program from executing the subroutine "one more time." If you follow

through the sequence of this program, you will notice that the
program will branch to the subroutine and return to the main
program three times.  After the third branch and return, the
program tells the computer to print the answer at lines 85
and 86.  If line 90 is omitted, the program will then continue
to line 100 and execute the subroutine again.  However, the
system will not know what to do with the RETURN and will
print an error message.  Notice that we must still use the
END statement to signal the last statement in a BASIC program.

A subroutine may be as complicated or as simple as required
in a program.  Also, a program may contain several subroutines
with one subroutine calling a second subroutine and then
returning to the first.

The general form of the GOSUB statement is

| 1- | Line number | Must precede all BASIC statements. |
|----|-------------|-------------------------------------|
| 2- | GOSUB | Key word that tells the computer to branch to the subroutine starting with the line number given in the GOSUB statement. |
| 3- | Line number | First line number of the subroutine. |

The general form of the RETURN statement is

| 1- | Line number | Must precede all BASIC statements. |
|----|-------------|-------------------------------------|
| 2- | RETURN | Key word that tells the computer to return to the first statement following the last executed GOSUB. |

The general form of the STOP statement is

| 1- | Line number | Must precede all BASIC statements. |
|----|-------------|-------------------------------------|
| 2- | STOP | Key word used to stop execution of the program. |

THE RESTORE STATEMENT

In some business applications, you may want to reuse data
from a DATA statement without having to duplicate the DATA.
We discussed lists and tables in Chapters 4 and 5 as one method
of storing data for repeated use.  However, BASIC gives
another method for making data available for reuse.

For example, assume we wish to calculate the mean of a group of data and then compare each data value to the mean. Whenever we find a data value greater than the mean, we want to print that value.  The program in Figure 6-5 will solve this problem.

```
 10   REM CALCULATE MEAN AND PRINT VALUES GREATER THAN THAT MEAN
 20   READ X
 21   DATA 25, 34, 27, 31, 29, 36, 40, 21, 42, 39, 28, 37, 41, 31, -99
 25   IF X < 0 THEN 50
 30   LET T = T + X
 31   LET C = C + 1
 35   GO TO 20
 50   LET M = T / C
 55   RESTORE
 60   FOR J = 1 TO C
 65   READ X
 70   IF M > = X THEN 80
 75   PRINT X,
 80   NEXT J
100   END
```

Figure 6-5

RESTORE Statement Illustration

## Explanation of BASIC Statements

In this program, the values from the DATA statement are read at line 20.  These values are accumulated at line 30 and counted at line 31.  When a negative value is found in the IF statement at line 25, all the data from line 21 have been used. The program branches to line 50 where the mean is calculated.

```
 55   RESTORE
```

The RESTORE statement at line 55 causes the original data from the DATA statement(s) to be recreated for processing just as if the DATA statement were repeated.  In this example, all data elements from line 21 are again available for processing. The RESTORE statement at line 55 has the same effect as the following:

```
 55   DATA 25, 34, 31, 29, 36, 40, 21, 42, 39, 28, 37, 41, 31, -99
```

Therefore, when the READ statement at line 65 is first executed, the first data element, 25, will be stored in X, etc.

The RESTORE statement will recreate data from one or more DATA statements. The order of the RESTOREd data is the same as the order of the original data specified in the DATA statement(s).

The general form of the RESTORE statement is

1- Line number      Must precede all BASIC statements.
2- RESTORE          Key word that recreates all data
                    specified in the program in DATA
                    statements.


FILES

Most BASIC systems give you a way to store or file output data from one program and to use these filed data in another program. In this type of processing, the data are stored in a file and retrieved from a file. We can define a file as a collection of data about one topic or subject.

A typical example of a business file is an employee master file. In this file, we would store all the pertinent data about each employee, such as employee name, address, social security number, dependents, rate of pay, gross earnings to date, and income tax withheld to date. This file would be used each week to prepare the payroll and would be changed each week to reflect the changes in gross earnings and income tax withheld.

We would also use this file each 3 months to prepare the reports to government concerning withholding taxes. And at the end of each year, we would use this file to prepare each employee's W-2 Form, which she will use to prepare her income tax return. As you can see, it is easier and more efficient to store data in files than it is to use DATA statements over and over again.

There is a great difference in the way you program BASIC systems when processing files. You should check with your BASIC programmers guide or with your computer center personnel to find out how your computer system works with files.

However, to give you a feel for file processing, Figure
6-6 is a simple program that creates a file and then retrieves
that file and prints the data stored in it.  This program was
written for an IBM 370 computer system using VSBASIC, but the
file statements are typical of many systems.

```
10   REM PROGRAM TO STORE DATA IN XFILE THEN TO RETRIEVE AND PRINT
11   REM DATA STORED IN THAT FILE
15   OPEN 'XFILE' OUT
20   READ X
21   DATA 25, 34, 27, 31, 39, 36, 40, 21, 42, 29, 28, 37, 41, 31, -9
30   IF X < 0 THEN 100
40   PUT 'XFILE', X
50   GO TO 20
100  CLOSE 'XFILE'
110  OPEN 'XFILE' IN
120  GET 'XFILE', X, EOF 200
130  PRINT X;
140  GO TO 120
200  END
```

Figure 6-6

Files Program

The first section of this program, lines 15 through 50,
read the values of X given in the DATA statement.  Each of
these values is then placed in XFILE one at a time.  The
second section of the program, lines 110 through 140, retrieve
the data from XFILE and print each data value one at a time.
New BASIC statements appear at lines 15, 40, 100, 110, and 120.
All of them are file instructions.

### Explanation of BASIC Statements

    15  OPEN 'XFILE' OUT

You must activate or OPEN a file before you can use it as
in line 15.  The file is named XFILE by the programmer.  The
file name may consist of from one to seven alphabetic or
numeric characters, the first of which must be alphabetic.
The file name is enclosed in quotes as shown above.

The word OUT specifies that XFILE is to be used for
receiving and storing data.  You can think of this output

process as "printing" data in XFILE rather than printing them
on a piece of paper.

If we wish to use XFILE to provide data to a program, as
input, we should use the word IN in the OPEN statement.  This
is shown at line 110 in Figure 6-6.

    40  PUT 'XFILE', X

This statement places each value of X into XFILE.  The
PUT statement is similar to the PRINT statement, but rather
than printing the values on a piece of paper, the values are
recorded in the named file.  If you want to store employee
data for the employee master file discussed above, you should
write the following statement:

    30  PUT 'EMPLOY', N$, A$, S, D, R, G1, T1

This PUT statement will store the employee's name and address
as well as her social security number, dependents, pay rate,
gross earnings to date, and income tax withheld to date.  All
these data will be stored in a file named EMPLOY.

    100  CLOSE 'XFILE'

If you have used a file as output and then wish to use
the same file for input, you must first deactivate or CLOSE
the file.  Line 100 closes XFILE.

    110  OPEN 'XFILE' IN

Remember, we want to use the data stored in XFILE as input
in this section of the program.  We must therefore open XFILE
as an input file.  Line 110 takes care of this.

    120  GET 'XFILE', X, EOF 200

Each time this statement is executed, one data value from
XFILE is entered in the CPU.  The GET statement is similar to
the READ or INPUT statement.  Rather than obtaining data from
a DATA statement, the GET statement retrieves data from the
named file.  You may include several variables after the file

name.  For instance, if you want to use the data stored in
file EMPLOY, you should write

    135  GET 'EMPLOY' N$, A$, S, D, R, G1, T1, EOF 250

This statement will enter these seven data elements into the
CPU for processing.

The EOF 200 in line 120 is a test for the end-of-file.
When there are no more data stored in the named file, the EOF
causes the program to branch to the line number given.  In
this example, the program will branch to line 200 after all
data have been retrieved.

The general form of the OPEN statement is

| | | |
|---|---|---|
| 1- | Line number | Must precede all BASIC statements. |
| 2- | OPEN | Key word which activates a file. |
| 3- | 'file name' | A programmer-supplied name which identifies a file.  May consist of up to seven alphabetic or numeric characters.  First must be alphabetic, and the name must be enclosed in quotes. |
| 4- | IN or OUT | Specifies whether file is to be used as input or as output. |

The general form of the CLOSE statement is

| | | |
|---|---|---|
| 1- | Line number | Must precede all BASIC statements. |
| 2- | CLOSE | Key word which deactivates a file. |
| 3- | 'file name' | See OPEN statement. |

The general form of the PUT statement is

| | | |
|---|---|---|
| 1- | Line number | Must precede all BASIC statements. |
| 2- | PUT | Key word which causes data to be placed in the named file. |
| 3- | 'file name' | See OPEN statement. |
| 4- | One or more variables | Specifies the data values created in a program that are to be stored in the named file. |

The general form of the GET statement is

| | | |
|---|---|---|
| 1- | Line number | Must precede all BASIC statements. |

| | | |
|---|---|---|
| 2- | GET | Key word which causes data to be retrieved from the named file. |
| 3- | 'file name' | See OPEN statement. |
| 4- | One or more variables | Names CPU storage areas in which data from the file will be stored. |
| 5- | EOF | Key word that tests for the end-of-file condition. |
| 6- | Line number | Point to which program branches when all data have been retrieved from the named file. |

## A BASIC Program as a File

When you are writing and using your programs in a time-sharing environment, your program is temporarily stored until you "log off."  It is then erased, and the only way you can use that same program again is to retype the statements on the terminal.  But you may have a program that you want to use over and over again without having to retype it each time.  Time-sharing BASIC assumes that your program is a file which you named when you "logged on."  You may type SAVE on your terminal, and the system will automatically store your program in some kind of permanent storage area.  Then when you want to use that program again, you can retrieve that file during the "log on" procedure.

## SUMMARY

In Chapter 6 we have presented several new programming techniques including standard functions, programmer-defined functions, subroutines, and files.  The RESTORE statement was also given.

Standard or built-in or library functions are supplied by the manufacturer of your computer system and are part of the BASIC language.  Each function performs a commonly used mathematical calculation.  Several standard functions are designed for trigonometric calculations, such as sine, cosine, tangent, and arctangent.  Others are for general mathematical calculations:  absolute value, exponential function, and natural logarithm.  Three other functions are especially

applicable to business applications:  integer part, square
root, and random number.  Ten standard functions and their
descriptions are presented in Figure 6-1.

You may only use a standard function in an expression as
follows:

. . . =  function name  (expression)

Programmer-defined functions are written only once in a
program and are used when one mathematical calculation must
be made several times in one program.  A programmer-defined
function has the following form:

line number  DEF  FN letter = expression

When the programmer wants to use a defined function, he uses
the function name, FN letter, in an expression in the body of
his program.

A subroutine is a mini-program consisting of a group of
program statements designed to perform several calculations
and to return the result(s) to the main program.  A subroutine
is used when the same set of calculations is to be performed
several times within a program.  The subroutine is "called,"
using the GOSUB statement.  Control is given back to the main
program using the RETURN statement.

A subroutine is "called" as follows:

line number  GOSUB  line number

The line number following GOSUB specifies the first statement
in the subroutine.

The RETURN statement is included in the subroutine and
returns control to the main program at the line number following
the GOSUB.

Many times it is necessary to use a group of data more
than once in a program.  Rather than retype the data in a DATA
statement, BASIC provides the RESTORE, which recreates the
original data in their original form.

line number  RESTORE

Another way to use data over and over again is to store

them in a file.  Most BASIC systems provide a method for file
processing.  However, because of the great variation in file
instructions, you should consult your computer center
personnel for the exact file instructions for your computer.


EXERCISES

A-  Correct any errors in the following independent statements.
Assume that all variables to the right of the equal sign have
been assigned numeric values.

    1-  LET INT(X) = A - B
    2-  DEFINE FSQR = INT((SQR(X - Y) - RAND(0)
    3-  PRINT FNQ(25)

B-  Write a programmer-defined function that will simulate the
roll of one die.  (See Figure 6-2.)
C-  Write the BASIC statement(s) that will replace lines 40
and 41 in Figure 6-2.  Use the programmer-defined function
from Exercise B.
D-  The following formula will convert X degrees to R radians:

    R = X * (3.1416 / 180)

Write a programmer-defined function to perform this conversion.
E-  You want to produce a multipage report.  Each page should
include a report title and page number as well as column
headings as follows:

                           CUSTOMER REPORT                         PAGE 4

    CUSTOMER NAME                                      ACCOUNT BALANCE

You should leave ten blank lines between the report title line
and the last detail line on the previous page.  Write a
subroutine to cause these headings to be printed.  Use proper
vertical spacing.

PROBLEMS

1- Write a program to print a table of values of X degrees for the sine X, cosine X, and tangent X.  X should range from 30 to 180 degrees in increments of 10 degrees.

Output      Column headings: DEGREES  SINE  COSINE  TANGENT
One detail line for each value of X.

Input      Create values of X within the program.

Process   Compute sine, cosine, and tangent.

2- There are 50 data elements to be entered into a 10 x 5 table.  These data should be random integers which fall between 5 and 25 inclusive.  You are to create these 50 data values and store them in a table and then print that table. Use a subroutine to accumulate the values in each row.  In the main program, print this total along with the word ROW and its number.  Then use the same subroutine to repeat the accumulations for each column.  The main program should print the word COLUMN with its number and then the sum.

Output      The created 10 x 5 table.
ROW, its number, the sum of the values.
COLUMN, its number, the sum of the values.

Input      Create within the program.

Process   Generate 50 values.
Sum each row.
Sum each column.

# Appendix A

# Simplified Keypunch Instructions

The numbers in parentheses which follow relate to the numbered components of the accompanying diagram of the IBM 029 keypunch.

a- Load the hopper (1) with cards. Any type of card, regardless of color or corner cuts, will work.

b- Turn the machine on if it is off. The switch (2) is located at the right under the table.

c- Press down the right-hand side of switch (3) so that the contacts are raised away from the drum [the contacts may be seen through the window (4)].

d- Turn all four center switches (5) up.

e- Push the FEED button twice. A card is now ready to be punched. Use as a regular typewriter for lower-order characters or letters. For upper-order characters (i.e., numbers and special characters), hold down NUMERIC.

f- The numbered wheel (6) indicates the number of the next column to be punched.

g- When finished with the punching of a card, press REL.

h- The next new card is now ready for punching.

i- If the keyboard locks (the buttons have no effect), press the ERROR RESET.

Source: Michael Kennedy and Martin B. Solomon, Ten Statement Fortran, Prentice-Hall, Inc., Englewood Cliffs, N.J., 1975.

j- When finished (or to clear the machine), flip the CLEAR switch (8).

k- It is possible, using the DUP key, to reproduce information in one card into another. Experiment with this feature to see how it works.

---

If you keypunch your own programs or data, there is a tendency to make use of some of those piles of "blank" cards which are inevitably left lying around keypunch machines. To do so is folly unless you check each card very carefully for punches. Someday, after you have saved $0.42 worth of cards for the environment, you may blow a $30 computer run and waste half a day of your time because a card wasn't quite blank.

---

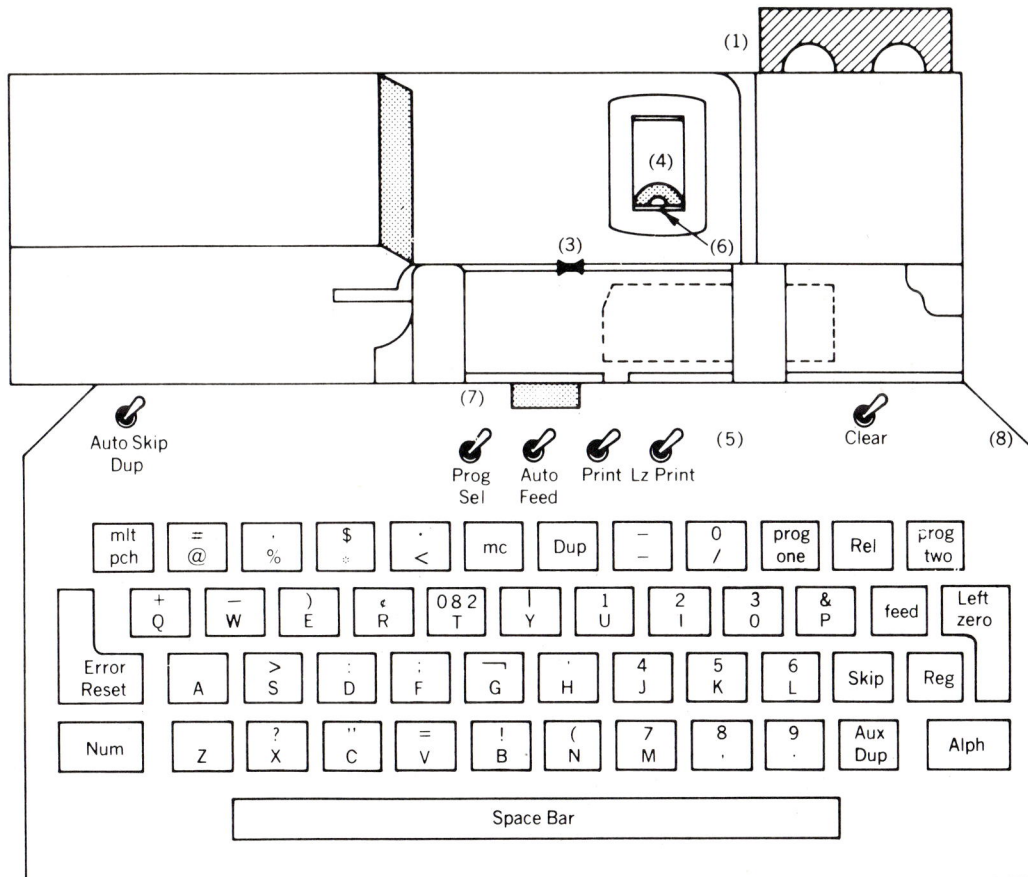

(2) not shown; switch under table on right hand side

# Appendix **B**

# **Batch Mode Job Control Language**

When you want to run your BASIC programs in a batch mode, you will use punched cards for entering your program and data into the computer. The job control language (JCL) will also be punched on cards and will tell the computer to run your BASIC program. Your JCL and BASIC cards will then be read by a card reader, which enters your program into the central processor.

We will use the Control Data Corporation job control cards as an example, but you will find that most systems that operate in a batch mode will use a similar JCL. These cards will be shown in the order that they must be entered into the card reader. The JOB card will be the first card read, and the 6/7/8/9 card will be the last card to be read.

JOB card | Specifies the job name, CPU memory, and time requirements.

BASIC card | Calls BASIC translating program.

7/8/9 | Separates JCL cards from your BASIC program (the 7, 8, and 9 digits are punched in card column 1).

Your BASIC program:

7/8/9 | Separator.

6/7/8/9/ | Specifies end-of-job (the 6, 7, 8, and 9 digits are punched in card column 1).

An example of a program deck setup is shown below:

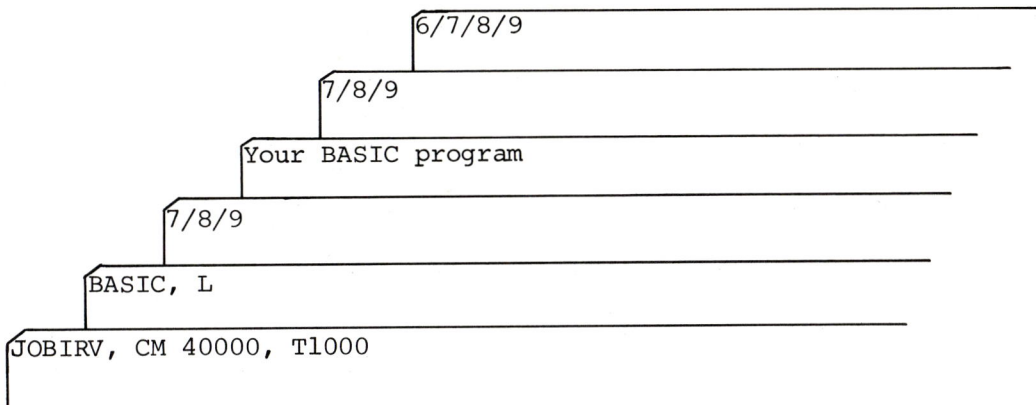

```
                                    6/7/8/9
                        7/8/9
                  Your BASIC program
            7/8/9
      BASIC, L
JOBIRV, CM 40000, T1000
```

# Appendix C

# Time-Sharing Mode Log On Procedure

When you are working with a two-device computer system, a terminal and a central processor, you will often be using a teletypewriter as the terminal. The teletypewriter will be both your input and your output device. When you want to use the teletypewriter terminal to run your program, you do the following:

1- Turn on the teletypewriter.
2- Dial the computer system telephone number (if the system is not directly connected to the terminal).
3- Log on.
4- Key your BASIC program on the keyboard.
5- Receive your printed output from the teletypewriter.
6- Sign off from the system.

These are the typical steps you follow when using any computer system in a time-sharing mode. However, the log on procedure differs from one system to another. We will discuss the Honeywell Series 400 BASIC as an example.

1- Turn the teletypewriter control switch to LINE. (The knob is located on the right-hand front of the machine.)
2- Push the TALK button on the data set. (This is a connector between the terminal and the telephone lines through which your terminal communicates with the computer.)

228

3-  Dial the computer telephone number.  When the computer
    is ready, you will hear a high-pitched tone.  Press
    the TALK button on the data set, and replace the
    telephone handset.

4-  The system will type USER NUMBER.  You will then type
    your number (given you by your computer center person);
    then press the RETURN key.  When using the teletype-
    writer, you will press the RETURN key after each line.

5-  The system then types NEW OR OLD.  You type NEW if
    you want to enter a new program, one that you have
    just written.  Or you type OLD if you want to recover
    a program you have used before and saved.  Don't
    forget the RETURN key.

6-  The system then types NEW PROBLEM NAME (or OLD
    PROBLEM NAME).  You then type any combination of
    letters and characters (not more than six) naming
    your new program.  If you are recovering an old program,
    you must type exactly the same name that was first
    given to that program.  RETURN again.

7-  The system then types READY.

8-  You now enter your BASIC program, starting each line
    with a line number and ending each line with the
    RETURN key.

9-  When you have finished your program with the END
    statement and the RETURN key, you can tell the computer
    to execute your program by typing RUN and then the
    RETURN.

10- After you are satisfied with your computer "run," you
    may save the program for future use by typing SAVE.

11- When you are finished using the system, you log off
    by typing BYE.

You will often make typing errors when using the teletypewriter.  You may correct these errors in several ways.  To
correct one or two incorrect characters, you depress the
SHIFT key and strike the letter O for each character you want

to correct.  Then you type the correct characters.  If you
want to correct an entire line, you simply retype the line,
using the same line number.  This will erase the first line
and replace it with the correction.

When you request an OLD program, you may want to be able
to examine that BASIC program.  You will have to tell the
computer to print out the program by typing LIST.  You may
also type LIST when you are correcting a NEW program.  This
will let you see exactly how your program is stored at that
time, after you have made several changes.

# Appendix D

# Debugging Your Programs

Whenever you try to run one of your programs, you will usually find one or more bugs (errors). One common type of bug is a language or syntax error. This type of bug is like a spelling or punctuation error in an English sentence. The other common type of bug is when your program runs and produces an incorrect answer. This is called a logic error. This is like using an incorrect formula when making a mathematical calculation. You did the arithmetic correctly but still got an incorrect answer.

Your syntax errors are usually easy to find and correct because your computer will print the number of the line in which the error occurs and will give you some hint concerning the kind of error. There is usually one message for each line that is incorrect. For example, suppose the following BASIC statements were in one of your programs:

```
25  LET A = B * (X - Y
30  PIRNT A
```

Your computer will print out two messages something like this:

```
PARENTHESES AT 25
ILLEGAL INSTRUCTION AT 30
```

From these messages, you can find the error(s) in each line and make the needed corrections and then try to run your program again. Each different computer system will use different messages, but they are easy to understand.

Logic errors, however, are more difficult to find and correct.  You should check each program you run to make sure there are no logic errors, as follows:

1-  Run your program to get computer answers.

2-  Calculate the answers by "hand," using the same data.

3-  Compare the computer and "hand" answers.  If they are the same, your program logic is probably correct.  If your answers are not the same, you have probably made a logic error.  Your problem is to find that error.  However, before you rush into finding your logic error, check your data.  Be sure you used exactly the same data for both your computer and "hand" calculations.

4-  Check your IF statements.  Look at your computer answers.  If one is larger than it should be and the others are smaller or actually zeros, you have propably made an error in one of your IF statements.  Think like a computer, and work your way through your transfer logic.

5-  Check your GO TO statements.  If your computer answers get larger and larger, you probably left a GO TO out.  Again, think like a computer, and work your way through the LET's and GO TO's.  Be sure you are not running two computations together.

6-  If you still do not find your error, tell the computer to print out all intermediate answers.  Do this by putting a PRINT statement in the loop.  The computer will then print out a series of answers that you can study.  You should then simulate the computer by making all calculations by hand and comparing each intermediate answer with the computer printout.  You might find that the first, second, and third answers are OK but that the fourth, fifth, and sixth answers are incorrect.  The fact that the first error happened at the fourth calculation should give you a good clue as to where the error is.

7-  Now that you have found the error, you should have
    no problem correcting it.

8-  IF ALL ELSE FAILS, DRAW A PROGRAM FLOWCHART.  THEN
    COMPARE YOUR PROGRAM TO THE LOGIC SHOWN IN THE
    PROGRAM FLOWCHART.

# Index